Liz Morrison

Simple Steps to Riding Success

Feel the Power of Positive Riding

Includes Exercises & Case Studies

David & Charles

*For Richard, my brother
(1957–2001), who lived his dream
and shared it with many friends*

A DAVID & CHARLES BOOK

First published in the UK in 2002
First paperback edition 2004

Copyright © Liz Morrison 2002, 2004

Distributed in North America
by F&W Publications, Inc.
4700 E. Galbraith Rd.
Cincinnati, OH 45236
1-800-289-0963

Liz Morrison has asserted her right to be identified as
author of this work in accordance with the Copyright,
Designs and Patents Act, 1988.

A catalogue record for this book is available
from the British Library.

ISBN 0 7153 1313 4 hardback
ISBN 0 7153 1820 9 paperback

Printed in China by Hong Kong Graphics & Printing Ltd.
for David & Charles
Brunel House Newton Abbot Devon

Visit our website at www.davidandcharles.co.uk

David & Charles books are available from all good
bookshops; alternatively you can contact our Orderline
on (0)1626 334555 or write to us at: FREEPOST
EX2110, David & Charles Direct, Newton Abbot,
TQ12 4ZZ (no stamp required UK mainland).

All photographs by **Kit Houghton** except the following:
Liz Morrison pp1, 95
Iain Burns pp4, 37, 98
Caroline Knight p8
Graham Wilson pp34, 91
Bob Atkins p39
Horsepix pp45, 55, 139
Emma Wilks p92
Bob Langrish p107

Contents

CASE STUDIES

Introduction

Choosing the right dream

Neuro Linguistic Programming (NLP) is a powerful psychological tool that can be used for building useful mental resources, clearing 'blocks' and setting goals – all skills that can revolutionise your riding. The most important factor in riding is our relationship with the horse, and this book shows you how to develop a calm and confident approach that can revolutionise your riding.

Developed in the 1970s by a linguist and computer studies expert, NLP now has a far reaching impact in many areas, including change-management in business, understanding the mind-body connection in health, acceleration of learning in education and positive mental attitude in sport. In most other sports, this subtle science has been understood for a long time as competitors who are equal to each other in physique, skills training and diet seek to optimise their performance through their minds. Now it is the subtle inter-relationship of the horse and rider that can benefit.

NLP is based on an understanding of how the brain and neurology works to influence memory and imagination. This is coupled with a focus on the language that we use to communicate both to ourselves and others – including horses. Verbal language reveals your motivations and beliefs and what you think about yourself, and body language, which horses can be particularly aware of, reflects how you feel unconsciously about many things. By understanding how our behaviour follows similar patterns and by recognising these patterns, you can predict and manage your response.

Using these three principles, NLP can be used to make fast, powerful and long-lasting personal change. It also provides an insight into the excellent performance and attitudes of others. Imagine being taught the exact behaviours and strategies of your hero and even being able to think the same way as he or she does. NLP can achieve this for you. And, as the case studies throughout this book demonstrate, adjusting one part of your life can result in significant beneficial change in other areas, too.

Working through this book

This is a practical guide to using NLP techniques to help you achieve your riding dream. It starts with exercises to clarify the goal you really want to reach. *Your riding dreams* helps you consider the implications of your dream so that you can be sure it is the right one for you. *Achieve your riding goals* sets you on the road to attaining your dreams by looking at your strengths and weaknesses and working out timescales. Everyone has different motivations and to achieve your goals you need to know what keeps you on track. Find this out in *Being motivated in your riding*.

One of the key aspects of achieving any dream is not only to know what you want, but also to have the beliefs that will support you in attaining your goal. Learn about the power of beliefs, how to recognise them and how to start changing them in *Believing you can ride better*. Beliefs are often deeply held and have been in place a long time so we are not aware of them. However, they shape our attitudes and behaviour and can limit us in what we do.

How our minds work and how to run them more actively or constructively is examined in *Understanding your riding inspiration*. For instance, notice the effect of waiting your turn to go into the ring at a competition. Compare it to the feeling of waiting to go out on a hack with someone, where there is no competitive pressure. Most people feel very different. Your response in the first instance is determined by your beliefs and imagination about what will happen in the ring. Your previous memories of that context will dictate how you respond to it.

The effect of what you say and how you say it is covered in *Talking yourself into riding well* and *change what you say about your riding*. *Improving your riding through your senses*, *Seeing yourself as a better rider* and *Making the most of your resources* take you through a variety of techniques that tap into the power of your memory and imagination, with exercises designed to help you get more out of your riding. Much of this book is focused on how to change. After all, logic says if what you are doing isn't working, then do something different! By helping you see things from a variety of perspectives, *Step into*

your horse's shoes gives you greater understanding of your horse, as well as other people. *Learning from excellent riders* is a series of studies on how 'those that can', do! *Making flying changes* explains some of the more advanced NLP change techniques.

Exercises

Throughout this book there are exercises. It is helpful to work through all of them, and some of the early exercises are best done for each of your goals (see p.13, for example). It may be an idea to copy them out and put them in a separate folder.

Case Studies

The stories of some of the many riders who have benefitted from NLP techniques are featured throughout to show just what is possible.

NLP Operating Principles

Here are some of the thoughts that have guided the development of NLP. They are discussed in more depth throughout the book. It is useful to act as if you hold these beliefs in order to utilise the techniques fully.

- We do not operate directly on the world, we create maps from our sensory experience, then operate from our maps. However the map is not the territory. And it is much easier to change the map than the territory. **(See p.55)**

- If you do what you have always done, you'll get what you've always got. **(See p.128)**

- There is no failure, only feedback. **(See pp.24, 26, 52)**

- All human beings share the same neurology: what is possible for one rider is possible for any rider. **(See p.104)**

- Your memory and imagination share the same neurological circuits. **(See p.75)**

- Wisdom comes from having multiple perspectives. **(See pp.96-7)**

- It is not what happens to you that makes the difference – it's what you do with what happens to you. **(See p.62)**

- You cannot not communicate – only choose to do so unconsciously or be conscious of the effects you create. **(See p.60)**

- The meaning of your communication is the response you get … which may be different from the one you intended. **(See p.54)**

- There is a positive intent behind all human behaviour. **(See p.60)**

- Energy flows where attention goes. **(See p.25)**

Your riding dreams

If you never have a dream
You can never have a dream come true
from the musical South Pacific

Make your dreams come true

It is possible…

read on to learn how

Most people have a **range of ambitions** for their riding or their relationship with their horse, but many never go further than just dreaming about them. However, **anyone can make their dreams come true**.

With an understanding of how your mind works, you can set the goals that are right for you and work out the steps to achieving them. This will lead to you getting even more enjoyment from your riding.

So, what is your dream with horses? A dream can be big or small, long-term or short-term, expensive or cheap, involve major changes or barely any. It can be a simple thing such as riding your horse past a spooky object, or a bigger issue such as qualifying as an international riding instructor. It can be short-term like wanting to jump a clear round, or long-term like being selected for the national team. What really matters is that you want it wholeheartedly. The

more you want it, the more you should be ready to make changes to get it. The bigger and more long-term and the more upheaval it requires, the more you need to be committed to it through the ups and downs on the road to reaching it. The joy of horses, and the journey with them, is that you will be learning all the way.

'My Horses, My Teachers' is a phrase that was coined by Alois Podhajsky, one time chief instructor of the Spanish Riding School. It sums up the reason you should dream your dream, and build up your knowledge and experience in the horse world – so that you can relate even better to the horse.

Typical dreams or goals

- To afford a new saddle or bridle
- To pass an equestrian exam
- To jump a clear round
- To increase my percentage score in dressage
- To learn to ride side-saddle
- To enjoy hacking out again
- To qualify for the championships
- To win the class today
- To be selected for the team
- To be able to keep my horses at home

Choosing the right dream

How can you be sure to achieve your equestrian dream? The answer lies in choosing the goal that balances with other areas of your life, using the techniques described here, and being prepared to make changes to achieve your goals. There is also another factor involved. Sometimes called synchronicity, or simply luck, it is about setting up your unconscious to achieve for you, too. Together these will ensure you achieve your desired outcome.

Change/work

The third step is change work. Very few goals can be achieved by doing exactly what you are already doing, so personal honesty is important to enable you to see what you need to change. This may involve increasing your technical skills or making psychological and emotional alterations. Examples of the first are to gain a deeper seat or attend special courses, or they may be more specifically physical, such as losing weight or becoming fitter. Psychological

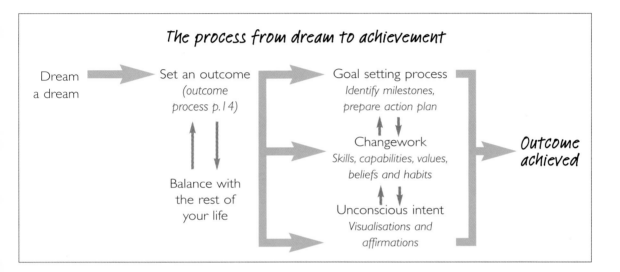

The process from dream to achievement

Dream a dream → Set an outcome (outcome process p.14) ↕ Balance with the rest of your life → Goal setting process *Identify milestones, prepare action plan* ↕ Changework *Skills, capabilities, values, beliefs and habits* ↕ Unconscious intent *Visualisations and affirmations* → **Outcome achieved**

Dream a dream and set an outcome

The first step is, quite simply, to know what you want. Do you? When it comes to pinning down a goal, other issues often pop up around it – they are all interrelated and so the task can become daunting. The outcome process (pp.14–16) is a simple but highly effective way of working out what you want and, most importantly, starting to understand the other issues that have an impact on it.

Set a goal

With a clear outcome, you can start the second step: the goal setting process (p.18). By working out all the milestones and action points along the way, goal setting helps you start to see the issues that may get in the way of you achieving your dream. It also starts the process of visualisation (see p.80).

and emotional changes might be improving your confidence, becoming more motivated or coping better with setbacks. Sometimes the aspects you identify as needing to change are interrelated – finding a more inspiring instructor or moving your horse to a more supportive yard, for example.

Unconscious intent

The fourth step, developing the unconscious intent (see p.24), will not work as effectively if your dream or goal clashes with other aspects of your life or if you are not prepared to make changes. When every part of you wants a goal, it is easy to start it happening.

Working through all these different steps is a commitment, and this book is designed to help you keep it.

Knowing what you want

Why having a clear outcome or goal…
is so important

Why is having a clear outcome or goal so important? After all it would be much simpler to wait and **see what fate brings along**, wouldn't it? Just accept your lot – it's easier than taking responsibility for what happens to you. Or you might think that if you don't have any expectations then **you won't set yourself up for disappointment**. If you agree with either of these attitudes, then this is fine – so long as you never feel fed up with your life or jealous of other people or generally behave as if you are hard done by. **Think again.**

It may be that that you have never needed to set goals before, or never understood their benefits. They are quite a recent phenomena. It was only in our grandparents or great grandparents time that people started to be able to influence their lives. Today, thanks to technology, the world is altering dramatically and at great speed and with these changes come previously unheard of opportunities.

Your mind generates actions based on
1 existing habits and reactions or
2 strongly motivating plans

This means that if you do not develop a strongly motivating plan, you will continue to do just what you have done before. Writing down your goals and the sub goals that you will achieve on the way is an excellent means of focusing your mind on what you want.

Knowing what is right for you
It is very important to be motivated by your bigger dreams, to really want to achieve them. Steven Covey, author of *The Seven Habits of Highly Effective People*, suggests imagining looking back on your life from a point in the future, say 10 or 20 years on and seeing whether the dream is still important to you (see p.20). After all, following it will be a commitment and a journey. How does it fit in with other important things in your life: family relationships, building a career outside horses, what you want to have achieved before you grow older?

Dream your own dreams

Don't be tempted to set goals that other people think are right for you or simply to keep up with your friends. When something is not right for you and your circumstances, it will **not** motivate you – in fact it may even become a source of stress.

Case study: Win the Hickstead Derby

When I was training with Rob Hoekstra a few years ago, he had just bought Lionel, who was talented but highly temperamental and so had been given up as 'not worth the effort' by other international riders. One day, as we looked at Lionel in his stable, Rob said to me, quite seriously, 'this horse will win the Hickstead Derby'.

It was a grand ambition: the Hickstead Derby is one of the world's most prestigious show jumping events, a highly competitive class that has had very few clear rounds in its history.

The year after we spoke, Rob was placed with only 4 faults. **The next year he won the class with the only clear round,** and the year after the pair jumped a clear round yet again. Normally, this would be enough to win and they took part in the most thrilling jump off to come third.

As a child, Rob had watched the Derby and he had vowed that one day he would win it. **He stayed 100 percent committed to his dream and he worked meticulously towards it.** He turned down other career paths, he trained hard, and he did not get sidetracked – other than to marry a supportive wife and start a family.

Our conversation and Rob's subsequent results demonstrate how knowing what your dreams are and being prepared to work towards them can help them come true.

Is it right for you?

Does your dream fit in…
with the rest of your life?

A benefit of using NLP approaches is that you find out **what is right for your life**. For example, you might be saying 'I want to ride at medium-level dressage and I'm not good enough' or 'I can't afford the horse or training', but **what you actually want is to enjoy greater harmony with your horse**. If the latter becomes your outcome or goal, you may well find that you can achieve it by going for rides in beautiful places or having lessons with a more classical instructor. If, on the other hand, you really do want to compete at medium-level dressage, you will be able to **see what you need to change or reprioritise** to achieve this. Are you prepared to forgo a holiday for your dream?

exercise

Exercise 1: Balancing different areas of your life

Take a few moments to dream and think about what you want in your life. In the boxes below, write down your first thoughts about each aspect. The box for personal development is where you take responsibility for what you need to do to make your outcomes or goals happen. You can choose to add your own headings.

Working through these top line goals and looking at the balance with different areas of your life acts like a reality check. You may realise that you are not prepared to give up work or change other aspects of your life in order to make your equestrian goal happen. You may find that you have more important priorities, like relationships or families, that you happily put first. By simply thinking about each area, you can choose to give yourself a break from nagging yourself for 'not having achieved' – because, after all, you have chosen something that is more important to you.

Horses

Home, Family and Friends

Work and Finance

Personal Development

Idle dreams

What about the times when something you wanted didn't happen or what if it hasn't happened yet? First, do you or did you really want that dream? Or did you immediately come up with a list of the reasons why you couldn't have it or didn't deserve it? The outcome process (p.14) will help you see where your dream did not fit with what another aspect of you wanted. (Believing You Can Ride Better, p.37, reveals where you may be limiting yourself.)

Exercise 2:
Combining your goals

This exercise helps you to see the common purpose that runs across many of your larger goals. It is also helpful to compare these results with your values, explored later (see exercise 13, p.49). The pyramid is constructed following steps 1 to 4. To help you, it is filled in with possible answers.

1 Pick four appealing goals from exercise 1 and write them in the boxes at the bottom of a pyramid, like the one below.

2 Choose a key word to summarise each goal and write it above your description of the goal.

3 Vividly imagine what it would be like to have achieved the goals in boxes 1 and 2. Ask yourself 'What does this do for me, get for me, give me?' Write the answer in the box above them.

4 Repeat step 3 for the goals in boxes 3 and 4.

5 Look at what you have filled in for steps 3 and 4 and ask yourself 'If I had these two things what would they give me?' Write your answer in the top box. Imagine what it would be like to have this now. Review each of the original four goals. Notice how it slightly adjusts your perception of them, and see whether one has become more important than the others.

Having these would give me
Belief that I can afford to invest in myself and so improve my riding even more

Having 1 & 2 would give me
A feeling of achievement and being recognised. I would know I can achieve bigger goals

Having 3 & 4 would give me
Determination to really make a go of my riding even while I have to work to pay for my horses

1 Horses
To win an intermediate event

2 Recognition
To get promoted at work

3 Health
To lose 10lbs and feel fitter than ever

4 Finance
To be able to afford to keep another horse

Internal goals

You can choose an external goal like jumping a certain course, qualifying for a competition or beating another horse and rider combination. Or you could choose an internal goal, one that's inside you. Internal goals tend not to compare your prowess with anyone else's and are also called process goals. They could be about creating a positive and resourceful state (p.86) so you feel more confident, overcoming a limiting belief (p.42) or simply getting to the show on time. On the whole, outside goals are beyond our control, but inside ones give you the chance of 'winning' whenever you decide to achieve them.

The outcome process
...get to the **heart** of what you want

To produce the **results you want, you need to know what you want.** The outcome process is a NLP technique for doing just this. It is a series of simple but carefully worded questions that **get to the heart of what you want.** Get into the habit of asking yourself these questions, and noticing the subtleties of your answers. It is a useful skill for talking to friends and colleagues about their plans, too.

Exercise 3:
Using the outcome process

Thinking about a goal you want, work through these precise questions – ideally with a friend – to see whether it is really right for you. Ask your friend to write down your answers *word for word* as you go along so that you can refer to them later.

1 What do you want?

Make sure your answer is positive by thinking of what you want rather than what you don't want – your friend can help you.

2 So if you could...would you take it?

Notice any doubts or extra comments like 'Yes, if...'. Where there is an 'if' or 'but', go back and redefine the answer to the first question to take these issues into account. You may need to do this 2 or 3 times.

3 Specifically, what, where, when, how do you want?

Phrase this question according to the content of your answer to question 1. Specify what you want, with as many details as possible.

4 When you have it, what will you feel, see and hear inside and outside of you?

Imagine what it will be like when you have achieved your outcome (your answer to question 1). Add in plenty of detail.

5 What will you do to achieve your outcome?

Think about the aspects of the outcome that are within your control. List the steps you are going to take.

`Cheshire Puss...´, said Alice,

`...would you tell me please, which way I ought to go from here?´

`That depends a good deal on where you want to get to,´ said the Cat.

`I don't much care where,´ said Alice.

`Then it doesn't matter which way you go,´ said the Cat*

* from Alice's Adventures in Wonderland Lewis Carroll

How do the questions in exercise 3 work?

The key is in the first question – the definition of what you want – and getting the answer into the positive. For example, 'I don't want to feel scared when I go out hacking' is not in the positive. Instead you need to develop it to something like 'I want to feel confident and calm when I go out hacking.'

Other examples might be:
'I want to afford to compete at elementary level.'
'I would like a career with horses so that I can keep my horse where I work and learn from professional riders.'

Why should it be positive?

Well, often we only know and talk about what we don't want, but imagine going to the supermarket with a list of everything you *don't* need that day. It would run into thousands of items! Think about shopping like that, having to check every item on every shelf. Apart from being inefficient it would be an overwhelming task. Positive thinking is effective because it is a more focused approach.

Thinking about your own example, you may find that as you come to pin down your goal, the issues around it become clearer. In the examples above the issues are about gaining confidence and continued learning. Knowing this helps you plan how to get there. Re-read the goals you wrote down (p.12) before going through the outcome process. Now can you see the other issues that are also part of them?

Check the 'ecology' of the solution

The second question checks the 'ecology' of the solution – is it really right for you? It may be necessary to go back to question 1 to define your answer even more precisely. For example, I have worked with people who say they want to compete at elementary level, but then when I ask them question 2, they have replied 'Well, yes, but I can't afford the lessons'.

These 'buts' and 'ifs' are often the real issues, which is why you need to go back to question 1 and redefine what you want. Question 2 from the example above

might be 'So if you could afford the lessons and costs of riding at elementary level would you take it?'

Notice the tone of your voice or your expression as you reply. They may reveal that you are not really committed. Move on to the next question only when you have a 100 percent positive response, because then the issues holding you back from this goal will have been brought into the equation.

Clarify the 'reality'

The third question adds more detail and clarifies the 'reality' that you want, specifying when, where, and with whom you want to achieve this outcome. In the example, the answer to question 3 could be 'To train my horse to elementary level within 6 months and be placed at an affiliated test within a year.'

Look into the future

The fourth question takes you into the future, to what it will it be like when you have achieved your outcome. This helps the dream to begin to develop in your imagination. Take time to think about all the details, even if they are guesses. Adding in the steps from the visualisation exercise (p.80) will make the image even more powerful. Writing it down is a useful extra step – later you will be amazed at how accurate that first visualisation was!

Taking steps

The final question helps you understand the steps you need to take to reach that desired outcome or goal. Write them down and put dates against them, too. Include even the most simple steps, such as ringing up to book a lesson. Think about the resources you already have. These may include instructors, friends and colleagues and role models. You probably have books, magazines and videos that can help you. You have your own personal resources such as concentration, calmness and determination. The techniques of anchoring (see pp.86–87) show you how to call up your personal resources again and again.

A well-formed outcome

Here is an example of some answers to exercise 3. It is quoted directly from one of my students.

1 What do you want?

'I want to be able to drive my pony on the roads where I live by December.'

2 So if you could drive your pony on the roads by December, would you do so?

'Yes, so long as I knew that we would both be safe, so I must take lessons and make sure that I am confident so that my pony will also be confident. Once I have done this and I am more certain of my abilities then I will be ready to take the next step.' So, if you can have all of the above, would you take it? 'Yes!'

3 Specifically, what, where, when, how do you want?

'Myself, my pony and an instructor will be involved, lessons will begin in June. After basic training, the first time I really drive it will be to the local park and back, which is a total of a one mile journey.'

4 What will you see, hear, feel?

'I will see my pony walking along in front of me in the sunshine on a frosty morning, there will be birds flying around and trees rustling in the breeze. I will hear his hooves hitting the tarmac, the sound of the cart wheels and the birds singing. I will feel the warmth of the sun and a light breeze. Inside, I will feel very excited and proud to have learnt a new skill.'

5 What will you do to achieve your outcome?

'The first step will be to research local establishments that can train me. I will read up on the subject so that I will be prepared for the lessons. Once lessons have begun, using an experienced horse, I will start to improve my pony's fitness. I also intend to take a series of exams offered by the British Driving Society. Then I will search for secondhand equipment so that practice can begin at home.'

Case study:
Karen gets a livery yard

Karen, aged 38, now runs her own livery yard and explains how using these NLP-based techniques has helped her.

'I used to teach IT, which I loathed. Worse, I ended up paying someone to ride my horses — and it was to keep horses that I was working in the first place! So I stopped working to concentrate on the horses and teach riding part time. However, this didn't add up financially. I was frustrated and losing my confidence.'

One of the biggest aims for Karen was to get her teaching business going.

see also:
What motivates you
ch.3
The Value of Values
p.48

Through the outcome process, she became more determined that this was what she wanted to do. 'Before I only had 1–2 lessons to teach a week, now I am kept busy with teaching and running my

yard, and I am able to afford to keep my horses, have training, and improve the yard to build the business.'

'Looking back I wasn't focused on getting pupils and giving lessons, I kept looking at different options to make ends meet. Using the outcome process meant I was able to pin down what I really wanted, so now I stick to one path and do it properly. I have advertised and feel more self-assured because I believe I can help my pupils — before I didn't really have that confidence.'

'I've stuck to it and I'm very positive about my future.'

Achieve your riding goals 2

If you are going to have a map, it's better to have one of where you want to go, not just where you are... *Robert Dilts*

Know yourself

'Most powerful is he who has himself...
in his own power.'*

Before you can draw up a detailed timeline for your goal and start working towards it, it helps to do analysis of your **strengths** and **weaknesses**, and any **opportunities** and **threats** that might exist. This will highlight where you need to **focus your efforts**.

Exercise 4:
SWOT analysis

1 Make a copy of the grid opposite. In the context of your goal, list your strengths in the left-hand box. Decide how important each is to your performance score (5 is high, 1 is low). Now write down what you can do to develop them even more.

2 Draw up a list of your weaknesses in the context of your goal – again these are factors in your control. Decide what impact each has on your performance and give it a score. Now write down what can you do to improve each one.

3 For opportunities think about the factors that are in your favour, a local reputation or good support from friends, for instance. Again score each and consider how you can boost these factors. It may be as simple as just thanking someone for being there to support you.

4 Now consider the threats or negative external factors you face. Score them and then consider what you can do to minimise them or cope with them better.

5 Finally, list the action steps (see p.22) that come out of this exercise. Then by looking at the scores you can put them in order of priority.

The example (opposite) supposes the goal is to take an equestrian exam. The two aspects that have most impact on performance (those with the highest scores) are self belief and lack of experience with strange horses, followed by a worry about wasting money and exam nerves. So the priorities here are to get experience on different horses, to find a positive instructor and to work on exam nerves. By identifying the strengths and weaknesses, opportunities and threats that are having the most effect on your performance, you can put effort into working at the things that will really make a difference. If you find that you can only work on one or two, choose those with the highest scores.

My strengths (things I am or can do)	Score	How will I develop this further?
Self.	5	Use instructors who boost my confidence.
My instructor says I am up to standard.	3	Check with another instructor.
I've got a good basic position.	3	Have lunge lessons to establish it even more.
I'm fit and slim so can look poised and elegant.	2	Make sure that I stay this weight or less.

My weaknesses (things I do)	Score	What can I do to reduce the weakness?
I tend to get exam nerves.	4	Work through exercises in this book.
My jumping position is crooked.	2	Keep doing grid work lessons.
I can get left behind when jumping.	3	Build up suppleness and experience.
I've only limited experience of riding strange horses.	5	Arrange to ride more horses.

Opportunities – external factors in my favour	Score	What can I do to build on each?
Intensive focus on my riding ability.	4	Make sure I enjoy lessons.
Recognition in the horse industry.	2	Be an active member of a national body.
A chance to work with competition horses.	3	Update my CV.

Threat – external factors which weigh against me	Score	How can I work around each?
The exam criteria may change.	2	Check with exam organiser.
It will be depressing if I fail.	3	Remember, whatever happens, I will have benefited from all the training.
It will be a waste of money if I fail.	4	Really focus on learning.

Know when you want it by

While working through this section, you may decide that **some goals aren't as important as you thought at first**. Some may not be really relevant to what you want to achieve. For instance, you think you want a dressage saddle. But your current GP saddle fits your horse, it just isn't a dressage saddle. And you want to event at riding club level so you don't actually need a dressage saddle. Do you genuinely believe a new dressage saddle will help to improve your riding? Or would working more often without stirrups or spending half the amount of money on a course of intensive lessons be more helpful? **Often we mistakenly think material things are the answer to all our problems**, fretting until we have them and then finding that our performance does not substantially improve!

The goal setting process is a very effective way to increase your motivation and measure your progress. It helps to highlight the skills you need to develop, and sort into logical order the tasks you need to undertake. Having a plan also shows you what progress you have made – so often we don't give ourselves credit for how much we've improved over a period of time.

It is best to start with the 'big picture', a timescale of at least 3–5 years for larger goals. Not all goals need to have an exact date – 'within a year' or 'by 5 years' is fine – although, obviously, riding championships or particular events have set dates that need to be worked towards. However, what really matters is that you are giving your unconscious mind a clear direction to follow.

exercise

Exercise 5: Establishing your timescales

The following exercise gives you an overview of the size and scale of the work required in achieving your dream and helps you understand your goals and what really matters to you.

Take each goal you have already identified (see pp.12–16) and think it through in terms of when you expect to achieve it. For each timescale, write down what you will have achieved. Use the two examples given on p.21 to help you create your answers. The white block illustrates when the goal itself is actually achieved. (The second example is from one of my students. By working back through time she identified what she had to do to be selected and six months later was placed at the European Endurance Championships.) Notice that the boxes start with the big one – 20 years in the future – as this gives you a better perspective on what you need to do. But if you feel daunted, start at a time when you will have achieved your goal, at least two years ahead, so that you are effectively looking back on what you need to do to accomplish it. Where your goals are shorter term, such as teaching your horse a new movement or qualifying for a championship, adjust the timescales to be closer together, say from two years down to next month.

When you work through this process, you may realise that plans that seem very important to you now are, in fact, quite short-term. Linking them in with your larger, broader goals gives them a sense of perspective. You may decide that you need to focus more on other areas of your life in order to achieve them.

Goal	To pass the Intermediate instructor's exam
In 20 years	To be respected as the instructor of riders who are now competing successfully.
In 10 years	To be acknowledged as a senior level instructor in my region.
In 5 years	To have taken next level exam. To be competing at the level, have a loyal clientele and to be enjoying teaching and mentoring a range of riders.
In 2 years	Have taken and passed Intermediate Instructor's Exam.
By next year	To increase number of clients through word of mouth recommendation. Feel ready to take exam. Have built experience competing at the level it relates to. Have selected exam centre and visited it.
Within 6 months	To have improved my jumping teaching through training with at least two jumping experts. To have started training as a dressage judge.
To do now	Identify jumping trainers to study with. Book dressage judges training seminars.

Goal	To be an international endurance riding champion
In 20 years	To be a leading trainer of endurance horses.
In 10 years	To be involved in developing the sport through my achievements.
In 5 years	To be world champion.
In 2 years	Selected for the world championships.
By next year	To have competed in an international trial.
Within 6 months	To have ridden well in front of the selectors and to have been selected.
To do now	Meet the selectors informally and demonstrate my commitment and ability. Get fitter so that my horse has the best chance of competing well at events. Keep to a training plan.

Make your goals happen

'There is no such thing as talent…
without great will power.'*

The next step is to **work out what you have to do to achieve your particular goal**. The longer term the goal is, the more likely it is to have milestones as well as action steps. **Milestones are events that will happen en route** to reaching your goal. They are achievements that also act as measures of your progress. For example, if your goal is to take a stable management exam, passing the mock exam is a milestone. **Action steps are the things you have to do to get there**, like learning the anatomy of the horse.

Case study:
Be prepared

From studying international riders and their grooms, and observing racing and polo yards (see modelling, p.104), I realised that they spend much more time planning, with more attention to detail, than I ever had.

They plan their outline competition programmes a year in advance, including dates for vaccinations, passport requirements, plans for their own holidays and rest breaks for the horses. They are also thinking about the progress of the less experienced horses. Their tackrooms and horseboxes are superbly organised: tack gets checked and repaired on time and all numnahs and rugs are clean. **At shows, the grooms know what tack to use, what time the horses will be competing and how much time is needed to prepare each one.** If the rider decides to change gloves, spurs or studs, all the spare equipment is kept ready at the ringside.

Martin Pipe, one of the most successful racehorse trainers in Britain, has an even more meticulous approach. He believes you can leave 'nothing, but nothing, to chance'. Behind everything he does there is research, logic and massive organisation. He says 'We are always improving what we do. Everything is for the

benefit of the horses. We're more scientific now, and blood tests allow me to understand the horses much more quickly.'

Such systems and efficiency are the hallmarks of high standards. And it is this that minimises error, ensures soundness and fitness and prevents accidents so that horse and rider can do their best. Because everything is so clear, changes can also be accommodated when they occur.

How does your organisation compare? Could your standards be higher? Imagine how much more you could enjoy a competition if you knew you were fully on track with your plan, allowed yourself enough time and that everything you needed was there!

* Honore de Balzac

Making lists

Consider the examples on the right and then list all the milestones and action steps for your own goal.

Within the action steps you can see that as well as tasks, there are usually skills and capabilities that you need to develop in order to achieve the goal.

Can you now identify how you need to develop and improve? This is the critical point where effective planning and goal setting starts. It is the more intangible elements, such as building confidence or motivation or attention to detail, that will really make the difference.

Using brainstorming

Use brainstorming to check you have considered all the aspects involved in achieving your goals – think of each and every thing you will need to do to complete them. It is often helpful to brainstorm with a friend.

Suppose your goal is to pass a riding exam. Start with a look at the elements you need to be able to do to pass the exam. Have you had enough experience in lungeing, feeding and fitness? Have you passed all the qualifying exams? Do you know the anatomy of the horse to the right standard? Are you confident of being able to cope with exam stresses? Have you spoken to other people who have taken the exam? How will you know you are ready? Can you arrange to go to the exam centre to ride before the actual day?

By brainstorming all the steps to passing the exam, you are creating a useful checklist. It is also a chance to dream up some solutions to the issues. Could you find a yard where you could offer to work at weekends in return for experience in lungeing or riding different horses on the flat? Could you offer to go to some shows as a groom in order to understand all about the procedures there? Could you invest in a week's intensive riding at a training centre before the exam?

Helping goals happen

Keep track of your goals and your progress towards them as this will motivate you to keep going. Tick off each action step as you do it and mark off when you

3 month goal
To enjoy cantering when riding out with friends

Milestones
- Canter around the field in a lesson
- Ride confidently past spooky items in the school

Action steps
- Watch instructor coping with spooky horses
- Improve my position and depth of seat
- Develop my confidence

12 month goal
To ride my best at the show jumping championships

Milestones
- Qualify for the championships
- Jump tracks at the championship height, confidently and clear

Action steps
- Ensure my horse is sound, fit and ready for the competition
- Enter qualifiers and book lessons
- Objectively assess areas for improvement with my instructor
- Check qualification requirements

3 year goal
To become a listed dressage judge

Milestones
- Complete all qualifying requirements before the exam
- Be invited to judge unaffiliated competitions locally
- Write for senior judges at affiliated competitions

Action steps
- Arrange to watch dressage horses training
- Attend at least two judges seminars
- Set up practice judging sessions
- Work on my ability to identify how a horse is going
- Learn test for the exam

Exercise 6:
Drawing up a timeline

By now you should have a list of milestones and action steps related to each of your goals. They can look overwhelming until you sort them out and prioritise them. This is the final step of goal planning: after this comes just doing it!

It is helpful to plot out your goal on a timeline (see below). Work on a large sheet of paper or on a computer spreadsheet. Draw a line across the middle, marking the left-hand as now, and the far right as the date by which you plan to have achieved your goal. Write the goal at the top, then the milestones you have identified, then all the action steps underneath, split into weeks or months. From this, you will start to see the priorities.

For example, suppose your goal is to take your riding exam within a year, but you lack confidence when jumping and haven't handled many strange horses, you also work full-time and have decided to spend extra money on training. The timeline could look something like this:

Planning for Your Goal: *To pass my level 2 riding exam*

Sub goals		Jump .90m course well	Gain more experience with competition horses		Get 55%+ in novice dressage	Jump 1m course well		Be told I could pass		Know I will enjoy it!	Pass!
Time	Month 1					Month 3					Month 6
Milestones	Get assessed	Start preparation for course	Book exam	Assist at five shows		Attend intensive training week		Pass mock exam		Visualisation	The Big Day!
Action steps	•Check exam dates •Plan exam preparation •Check out evening courses	•Find yard to help at •Check syllabus	•Book training week •Plan shows to watch at	•Book extra jumping lessons	•Identify knowledge gaps	•Arrange mock exam	•Practice lungeing	•Book extra position lessons		•Revise feeding	•Check exam day clothes fit! •Revise fitness

reach the different milestones. You could plan in little achievement rewards for yourself, too. With smaller goals is enough to have a record in a notebook. Display really important goals and share them with your friends. Discussing the ups and downs on the way will encourage you to keep going towards your goal.

There is no such thing as failure...

Remember that no goal achievement or learning is ever an upward-only curve (see pp.28–29). When there are setbacks and delays, it is useful to consider what you have learnt and what you would do differently next time. It is always OK to adjust the plan in the light of this new information. What

matters is that you continue to develop and learn through the goals you have set with your horses.

You don't have to try so hard

Have you ever said something like 'I wish I could ride like that' or 'I want to keep my horses at home' or 'I'd love a new saddle'? And then looked back some time later and realised your wish had come true? What did you do to make it happen? Maybe nothing. Because just by focusing your unconscious attention on what you wanted, you began a process that made it happen.

The brain is a 'cybernetic mechanism' — once you are clear about your outcome, it will start to organise all your unconscious behaviour in order to attain it.

The part of your brain called the Reticular Activating System (RAS) screens out everything except what you need to survive and progress. It acts like a magnet, attracting the information and opportunities that can help you achieve your goal. Once you know what you really want, your unconscious mind starts to adapt and adjust your behaviour to move closer to your goals. It will even unconsciously start giving self-correcting feedback to keep you on track. Being able to switch on your ability to achieve what you really want, simply by thinking about it, sounds dream-like, but it has been proven. For example, the success of self-healing, where someone who is ill decides to focus on becoming well, is well documented.

Increased awareness

Once you know your dream is right for you, you might notice that you keep seeing little prompts of it. This is because your memory and imagination share the same neurological circuitry. In addition, you may see pictures and read articles about it, hear people talking about it. You may meet other people who have what you want. If you stay committed to that dream, these are all signs that you are focusing on what you want. You can help to reinforce the dream by talking about your ambition to friends, by keeping pictures that show your progression towards it and taking the time to do frequent visualisations (p.80).

Using affirmations

Don't be tempted to set goals that other people think An affirmation is much more than an unbelievable statement that you repeat endlessly to yourself. To say 'I am a good rider' will not be convincing until you consistently and deeply believe it. It is much better to ask yourself a question such as 'What can I do today that will improve my riding?' or 'What can I do now to understand my horse better?' This will give you a much more emotional state. See also exercise 18, p.66.

When you have developed your affirmation, do not repeat it to yourself automatically. Really think about it, believe it, want it, make it in the present as if it were happening – NOW! Create triggers to remind you, perhaps position a picture with the words underneath it on the fridge door, in the car or on the top of your tack box. Then begin to act as if your affirmation was true – imagine what it feels like to be a really good rider!

Case study: To be a world champion

Reiner Klimke spoke about the lengths he went to make Ahlerich a European, World and Olympic Champion.

During the build up to the World Championships in 1982 (his goal), he realised that the existing champions, Christine Stuckleburger with Granat, would have the assets of sentimentality and the home crowds on their side, he also knew that the president of the jury would be Gustav Nyblaus, who had not liked Ahlerich in the early phase of his career. So **he knew that he had to convince Nyblaus** (a milestone) **in order to win**.

Therefore, Klimke followed Nyblaus wherever he was judging (the action steps) so that **he would have the opportunity of observing Ahlerich** and become convinced of the horse's consistency and brilliance.

It was as a direct result of his work that Klimke succeeded in his goal and became World Champion.

Learning from thrills and spills

'It's not whether you get knocked down, but whether you get up.'*

Only a few generations ago, almost everyone had daily contact with horses and being able to ride was an accepted part of life. Today most **people have to choose to learn how to ride**, and learners might have lessons perhaps just once or twice a week, often on a different horse each time. Because riding and horses are not so much a part of everyday life, **experiences from other areas of our lives can spoil our ability to improve and act with confidence** in our riding.

Over the last century the rate of change in the way we live has speeded up – and our ability to cope and respond needs to match it. NLP is a way of teaching the brain to have more choices about how to respond to a situation, rather than letting unrelated old responses and attitudes, such as fear or tension, get in the way. And, indeed, we can be subject to outdated beliefs handed down from generation to generation, about what is dangerous or what is appropriate behaviour.

Understanding how we learn is useful in helping us to make all our learning as effective as possible, and to manage the 'disappointments' and 'set backs' that may occur along the way to achieving our riding goals. Adults can be impatient to learn everything at once, but it's been recognised that this doesn't work. Instead, we need to build on what we have experience of, stacking each new skill onto the last.

Unconscious and conscious learning

Studies show that with any subject or skill, the way we learn is always the same: we start by not being aware of how little we know (unconscious incompetence), to knowing how little we know (conscious incompetence), to accepting our new-found knowledge (conscious competence) and, finally, to taking it for granted (unconscious competence).

Unconscious incompetence
'Let's go for a ride, after all it looks so easy, and horses are so lovely!'

A beginner starts learning about horses, assuming that one sport is going to be much like another and having only a basic idea of the skills required. At this stage, the focus is on clothes and tack – looking the part (environmental factors). This is not just relevant to beginners, though. It happens whenever we learn a new skill, such as starting lateral movements or entering our first affiliated show.

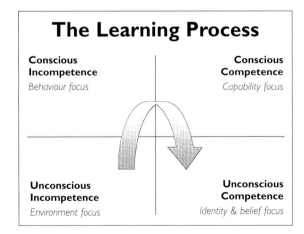

The Learning Process

Conscious Incompetence	Conscious Competence
Behaviour focus	*Capability focus*
Unconscious Incompetence	**Unconscious Competence**
Environment focus	*Identity & belief focus*

When to ask for help

Always seek good qualified instruction from the very beginning. Don't wait until you've have had a setback and your confidence has been knocked. Because we think it is easy, we often don't seek external advice or correction at the unconscious incompetence stage. Instead, we wait until the conscious incompetence stage, when we have learnt that it is not so easy as it looks.

Conscious incompetence

Once we start learning the new skill, progress is continual, but slow. Aware, now, that it isn't as easy as it first looked, we feel very motivated and want to learn more about how to behave and what to do, and so we spend time watching, listening, asking questions and reading. Now our language illustrates that we know we don't know it all 'I'm just a beginner', 'I can't think about keeping my head up, and my heels down, and my hands forward all at the same time.' We tend to seek external approval and direction, frequently asking 'Is that right?'.

Conscious competence

Our skills are developing fast – we can look back and see and feel the improvement we've made. Our instructor doesn't have to say the same things over and over again. Although it's still challenging to concentrate on the different aspects of our riding position at the same time, our coordination improves. We know how much we know, and also that there is more to learn. The focus is on establishing more skills and capabilities, perhaps moving on to improving the contact and sitting more softly.

Unconscious competence

We eventually reach the stage where we have good skills and, for the most part, can apply them without thinking. We can understand what to do to ride in a relaxed and safe way and are at ease in the environment of horses and riding. We are operating more at 'belief' level: 'I can ride, I can do that, this is easy.' The more we operate unconsciously like this, the more 'mind space' we have to learn other skills and improve further.

Then, guess what? We decide to learn a whole new skill, such as lateral work, and go back to the beginning of the cycle again, back to unconscious incompetence.

Motivating yourself through these phases and handling setbacks, is an important aspect to consider when planning how to achieve your goals (see pp.20–25 and *Thinking riding* pp.46–47).

Exercise 7:
Your achievements

exercise

We've all achieved many things, coped with difficult circumstances, learnt seemingly impossible tasks, yet we tend to take all this for granted. Think about all the things you've learnt or done starting with learning to walk, learning to talk, riding, passing exams, getting a job, using a computer, driving a car, and include more personal successes like overcoming adversity. List at least 30 things you have learnt and achieved. Put a star beside the ones that appeal to you most.

Keep referring to this list, and adding to it, and take a look at it any time you start to tell yourself negative things about your abilities (in NLP, what your internal voice says is called self-talk). We'll come back to this list for some exercises later, too.

Expectations and performance

There is a relationship between what we hope to achieve and our performance. Albert Bandura, a Stanford University psychologist, found that what we expect to achieve matters much more than what we achieved before. And that future performance can't be predicted purely on the results of similar past experiences. What counts is how positive we are in our approach to a new situation. For example, if we do something expecting to do it well, we will probably find that we will do it well, and will see any failure or problem as just a temporary blip. We've all met the 'precocious' child who says 'Oh, yes, I can do that' and does. And the fearful one who says 'I don't think I can do that' or, more likely, 'I don't want to do it', and doesn't do it well. Is the precocious child wrong and too ambitious – or just exhibiting what should be a normal optimism; how did the fearful child pick up or learn his or her reluctance?

Tapping competence

Competence is something available to all of us, but we do not always tap into it because of our beliefs about ourselves. However, anything that boosts our expectations can give us a period of unconscious competence, when a new skill seems easy. This is like the 'placebo effect' in medicine: when a patient is unknowingly given a placebo instead of medicine, they expect to feel better so they do. The expectation triggers latent competence in the immune system. Yet the placebo could not have had an effect of its own. Maybe this is why we often ride better after a change of bit or with a new saddle!

Bandura Curve 1

Albert Bandura developed a graph to show how progress in any skill follows a set route. As we begin to learn (unconscious competence) and our expectations of our performance rise, we improve, but a little slower than we expect. So our expectations of our abilities stop growing – this is the point of unconscious incompetence. As we approach conscious incompetence, our efforts falter and our performance is less good. We notice the relapse and feel despondent: 'Why am I doing worse than when I began?' Now, the difference between our expectations and our results is greater than at the start. A crisis develops. However, by recognising the situation and making adjustments, we can reach the level of conscious competence and make progress again.

For example, suppose someone goes on a diet. If they really expect to lose weight, they will mobilise all sorts of competencies – sensible levels of exercise, better eating habits, eschewing 'junk' food. They should begin to lose weight, but eventually there will be a plateau. Weight loss slows down, and old bad eating habits can re-establish themselves and their weight creeps up again. They will need to adjust their behaviour to progress…

Making adjustments

Ask yourself the following questions:

- 'What is the situation I am seeing as a failure?'
- 'How have I progressed since, say, 2 years ago?'
- 'What can I learn from this experience?'
- 'What would I do differently if it happened again?'

For example, if you are training for a riding exam, you may need to re-read your notes and books in more depth to make maximum use of what you are learning in the saddle, or it may help to repeat some topics with a different instructor.

New identities

When you find you need to make adjustments, you may also realise that you have reached a point of no return. It may be that you can no longer say 'I'm just a beginner.' (See also logical levels, p.46.)

If this new 'identity' makes you uncomfortable or it conflicts with your other identities, your performance may falter. Avoid this by thinking about the positive benefits of your old identity, and about ways in which its skills can be fitted into your new one. For example, tell yourself 'It was great being at riding school because there was always someone there to check

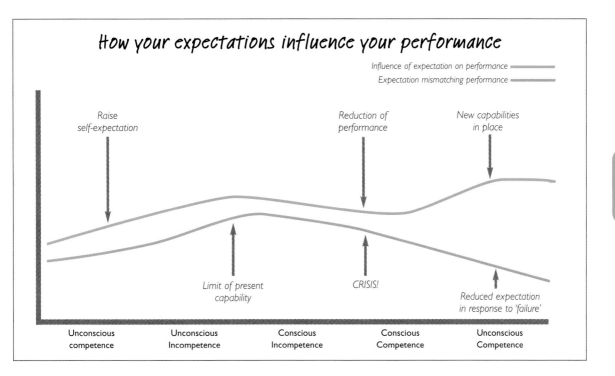

How your expectations influence your performance

Influence of expectation on performance ▬▬▬
Expectation mismatching performance ▬▬▬

Raise
self-expectation

Reduction of
performance

New capabilities
in place

Limit of present
capability

CRISIS!

Reduced expectation
in response to 'failure'

Unconscious competence	Unconscious Incompetence	Conscious Incompetence	Conscious Competence	Unconscious Competence

everything was OK and I could always ask questions. Now I have my own horse, I need to make sure that I can afford regular lessons, keep learning and ask the yard owners their advice if I'm not sure. It's OK to still be a learner as a horse owner.'

Your new identity will bring with it a whole new level of unconscious competence, and the cycle begins again. You may have to go through a process of trial and error to move on. Regression or relapse is quite usual. An example of this is a beginner rider having trouble with rising trot after learning sitting trot and canter.

Bandura Curve 2

Sometimes there is a difference between our expectations and our performance, the second curve on the graph shows this. We may see the 'crisis point' as 'failure' and lower our expectations, thinking 'Oh, this won't work. I'm useless.' And as our performance drops, our expectations lower even more, and we might regress back to below our starting level. For example, as the beginner dreads the thought of sitting trot or canter, they tense up, bump around even more and their hands rise as they lean back. At this point encouragement by others may be

counterproductive. Cries of 'Go on, you can do it!' may be met with 'OK, if it's so easy you do it!' Encouragement of a different kind is needed (see pp.31–36 about what motivates you to understand what is the best instructor style for you).

Learning from experience

You don't need to know all the theory before learning something. Think back to your childhood. No one taught you about the anatomy of the foot, the optimal sequence of footfall, weight transfer and the physics of balance before you walked – did they? This explains why you can't learn how to ride without getting on a horse. Words and descriptions are not enough – you need to experience the different sensations through as many of your senses as you can. It also reveals why it is so valuable to ride well-schooled horses at frequent stages of your learning. After feeling what a smooth jump is like, or the softness and balance of a good transition, or even the flow of a good half pass, your mind will be able to look for parallel feelings when you ride the same movement on a more difficult or inexperienced horse.

Case study: British Racing School

The benefit of learning well from the beginning is demonstrated by the work of the British Racing School, a charity that trains young people for the horse racing industry.

In just six weeks new recruits, who have usually had no experience of horses, will be able to look after young thoroughbreds and ride them on the gallops. **The training is intensive.** Recruits have to look after two or three horses to a high standard and tight deadlines, as well as attend lectures. **By the end of the first two weeks in an indoor school the riders can walk, trot and canter with short stirrups, balancing through their body weight without depending on the reins.** The next two weeks are spent on a circular gallop, where pupils get their first experience of lively behaviour and the power of a full gallop. The last two weeks are on the straight gallops, with the instructors driving a car beside the track. Each rider has a headset through which they receive personal instructions.

The teaching methods demonstrate some of the principles behind accelerated learning. The first is the need for 'towards motivation' – the youngsters want to work with racehorses, and are guaranteed a job if they pass. The second is the need for a high level of personal supervision – each week the young jockeys are given a review of their standards and what they need to demonstrate during the following week. This is also an example of very immediate goal setting, with no scope to slip. The level of personal interest is in stark contrast to what they experienced at school, and the results are impressive. **There is a very low failure rate.** After six weeks most of the riders will be able to ride racehorses; they will also have lost weight, become fitter and have learnt about timeliness and professional standards.

No amount of reading books and watching videos will make up for time spent in the saddle, if you really want to improve, work out how could you spend more time riding.

Second nature

The more we practise a skill or repeat a sequence of activities, the deeper it is instilled, until it becomes an unconscious process. This is why it is so important to be learning the correct things, because we can instill bad habits or negative beliefs just as easily. For example, it is vital that early riding lessons are safe and supportive, so that the new rider has had plenty of good experiences before the virtually inevitable fall occurs. Too many people tell me that they rode once and it wasn't for them – they then recount a horror story of going out with more experienced friends, the horses taking off, not being able to stop and even of falling off. For a first-time rider, a horse in walk can feel out of control. There they are six or seven feet up in the air, knowing that this animal has a mind of its own and they have only these thin leather straps to control it with. (Remember your first time driving a car – how fast 20mph felt when you hadn't worked out the steering or the synchronisation of clutch and gear lever?) Meanwhile their well-meaning friend or novice instructor wants them to experience the fun of trot and canter in the first lesson. No wonder so many find an excuse never to get on a horse again.

Being motivated in your riding 3

If I do not practice one day I know it.
If I do not practice the next day the orchestra know it.
If I do not practice the third day the whole world knows it.

Ignace Paderewski

What keeps you going?

Do you prefer to be told you are riding well…
or do you just know?

Are you **proactive or reactive**? Are you **internally or externally referenced**? Are you **attracted to achieve goals** or **motivated to avoid problems**? Do you **think big or need the detail**? You can answer all these questions simply by looking at the language you use. We unconsciously filter and modify the information we receive to make sense of it and to communicate it to others. Our individual filters are determined by our experiences, our culture and our belief, so we each see, hear and feel things in a unique way. **The way we live** (our daily habits) **reflects** our preferred learning styles and **how we are motivated**.

Our language is structured into habitual and identifiable patterns, which NLP refers to as 'meta-programmes'. These can be used to learn how to motivate yourself. They can also help you choose the types of people who will support you most in achieving your riding goals (see exercise 8, opposite).

Recognising and making use of meta-programmes will improve your communication skills. Without them, it can be like speaking to someone in a different language: it's not that you can't understand or that the other person can't communicate, but simply that you both operate differently. (See also pp.68–71.)

Motivation for Karen

Karen, who found the goal setting exercises so valuable in turning around her livery and teaching business (see p.16), also found the following exercise a useful insight into motivation.

'Because I hadn't gone on with my training, I believed that there were other teachers around who were better than me, and that I didn't have anything special to offer. Learning about how people are motivated helped me see that different people need different teaching styles and that I can build better relationships with people if I think about what would motivate my pupils and adapt my style more.'

Think big? Prefer detail?

When you learn do you prefer the 'big picture', or do you enjoy going through lots of information? Big picture people can be identified by their use of words and phrases like 'in general...', 'the important thing is...', 'take a wider view...'. Meanwhile detail people give plenty of information when they talk to you, using words like exactly, precisely, specifically. By simply noticing the level of information that someone prefers and giving them that amount back, you can motivate and build good rapport with them.

Exercise 8:
How are you motivated?

Get a friend to ask you the following simple questions. Answer them freely and spontaneously, writing down your answers word for word. Then read through the sample answers given on pp.34–36, and carefully re-consider your own answers to choose which of them is most like your own.

As you read about motivation styles, remember no single style is good or bad, it is just preferred by that person. By matching styles and developing flexibility between them, you will get better rapport and greater understanding of other people.

1	How do you know you have ridden well?
2	Why did you choose this goal?
3	State your goal and ask 'What is important to me about this goal?' Note your answer and re-ask the question. Repeat two or three times.
4	What is the relationship between your riding now and what you have achieved in the past?

How do the questions in exercise 8 work?

1 How do you know you have ridden well?
Your answer to this question reveals whether your motivation is internal (self-motivated) or external.

- a) I'm worn out but I know my horse has gone well and we have improved.
- b) My instructor is really pleased with us.
- c) I don't really know, but I imagine that if we were doing a test there would be some good marks.
- d) I know my horse has gone well, but it is also great to hear everyone say 'that was a good test'.

Answer a) is about internal references –
the feeling of being worn out and knowing inside that your horse has gone well. If you are an internally referenced person you decide about the quality of your work and are less likely to accept someone else's opinions and rules. You are less open to advice if it conflicts with what you already believe, especially if it is from a new instructor. This may make it more difficult for you to unlearn bad habits! An internally referenced person prefers to hear words and phrases like 'consider', 'here's a suggestion for you', 'what do you think', and being given an opportunity to relate lessons learnt to their previous experience. In terms of goal setting you probably won't see the point of discussing your progress and goals with other people – you know how you are getting on!

Answer b) is about being externally motivated –
at the extreme it takes an instructor telling you or seeing a score to know how good your performance was. If you are an externally motivated person you need other people's opinions to know how well you are doing. This can make you feel quite vulnerable when competing at a higher level where there is less positive feedback. When schooling a horse on your own, you are more likely to get de-motivated and to lack direction. You will be more motivated to achieve your goals if you talk to your friends about your progress and keep a chart.

Answer c) is an example of how an externally motivated person allows for not having someone to guide them – they imagine what someone else would say.

Answer d) is a combination of both types.
The one that comes first, in this case internal, is the marginally dominant style.

You can also be at any point between two extremes and your profile may vary in different contexts: for instance you might be internal when working with an instructor for the first time, and external when competing.

2 Why did you choose this goal?
Your answer to this question reveals how you approach a situation.

- a) I knew my horse was good so I took lessons, competed through the levels, qualified and now want to do my best in the class.
- b) The national championship is a fantastic occasion, my horse deserves the recognition, and my parents would love me to qualify to ride in them.
- c) Ever since I was a child I wanted to ride in the national championship. Each horse I have owned has taken me closer to it, so it has always been my dream and now I know I can achieve it.

Answer a) has a sense of history about it, it is telling the story of the steps taken to choose the goal. This is called the **procedures** style. If you are a procedures person you prefer to work logically, following an established route. You prefer a clear step-by-step approach – first you do this, then you do that, and so on. Words and phrases such as 'orderly', 'logical', 'this is the right way', 'it's tried and tested' are used. You are good at ensuring nothing is missed.

Answer b) is the opposite to a), giving a list of several of the different reasons why the goal

was chosen. It is called the **options** style. As an options person, you are motivated by opportunity and possibilities – 'better ways of doing things'. You like to generate different solutions to the same problem. You are motivated by words and phrases such as 'break the rules', 'opportunity', 'choice', 'here's another way of doing it'. You are good at developing new ways of doing things, rather than sticking to routines.

Answer c) is a combination of procedures and options, flexibility in both styles.

These are very different styles: options and procedures people find each other frustrating to be with in many contexts, but they sometimes need each other! When someone is first learning a skill, it may be better to teach in procedure language, then adapt subsequent sessions to their individual style. When choosing an instructor, however, choose someone who matches your style. That way you will enjoy your riding more.

3 *State your goal and ask 'What is important to me about this goal?'*
Ask the question two or three times. By re-asking the question, you reach deeper levels of criteria (to learn more about this see exercise 13, p.49). Your answers reveal whether you go towards or away from motivation – popularly known as the carrot and the stick!

• *a) I want to qualify my horse for the regional finals.*

It would demonstrate that I have trained him to a good level.
I enjoy training him.
I believe he is a good horse and it would show people how talented he is.
• *b) I want to qualify my horse for the regional finals.*
I want people to know that I am good enough to train horses.
I need to earn my living from training.
Otherwise I'll be broke and have to give up.

Answer a) is typical of someone who moves towards motivation (the carrot). The subsequent answers are positive, leading to achieving higher goals, dreams and aspirations. If you are 'towards motivated', you need to find an instructor who talks in the positive about what you will be achieving, using words and phrases like 'what you will get', 'how to achieve'. Very towards motivated people are so focused on what they want that they may not notice what will stop them, and so fail to plan on how to avoid potential obstacles.

Answer b) reflects the outlook of someone who prefers to move away from problems (the stick). If you are an 'away from motivation' person, you are activated by the thought of what will happen if you don't do this or that. You cope well with problem solving and are often good at crisis management and avoiding obstacles. However, you are less able to focus on long-term goals than towards motivated people and are more likely to respond to words and phrases like 'avoid', 'steer clear', 'get rid of', 'if you don't do this, this will happen'.

On the whole, 'away from motivation' is more stressful than 'towards motivation'. If you spend your life thinking about all the things that could go wrong it means you are spending a lot of time and energy dreaming up horror movies that may never happen. However, away from motivation can be utilised to drive you from a situation or really push you into changing a habit (see exercise 34, p.132).

4 What is the relationship between your riding now and what you have achieved in the past?

Your answer reveals how you react to change and the frequency with which you need change. It is one of the most useful things to recognise about yourself.

Do you like sameness in your life or plenty of gradual improvement, or are you one of those people that can't resist the latest 'new improved' approach? How easy is it for you to change instructors, livery yards, even horses? A word of caution: often people needing a high degree of change in one area of their lives, such as work or changing horses or livery yards, will have marked stability elsewhere, such as in their relationships or their home address. When you consider your answer, it is important to be clear which aspect of your life you answered about.

- a) It's the same really, I just like to enjoy my horse and ride at shows now and again.
- b) Well I'm more confident and beginning to improve, I'd just like to develop my position so that I can jump a course well.
- c) I've got a different horse and a new instructor, so I'm determined to really make a big difference to my results this year.
- d) I'm much more determined to improve my results and so I'm going to change my instructor and spend more on training to get a better position so that it'll really make a difference this time.

Answer a) is typical of a sameness person. If your answer is like this you do not like change and may refuse to adapt. You like the world to stay the same. While you may accept change every 10 years, you will only provoke it every 15–25 years. To identify this preference look for words such as 'the same as', 'in common', 'as you always do', 'like before', 'unchanged'.

Answer b) indicates a sameness with exception preference. In your answer, look for words such as 'more', 'better', 'less', 'same except', 'evolving', 'progress', 'gradual improvement'. You like things to mainly stay the same, preferring your situation to evolve slowly over time, so you will resist major changes unless you perceive them to be gradual. You need change once every 5 to 7 years.

Answer c) is an example of a difference person. If your answer is close to this one, you love change, often wanting it to be constant and major. You actively resist static situations and will often initiate change. You need drastic change every 1–2 years. In a work situation, difference people may leave a job if they do not experience enough change. Look for words such as 'new', 'different', 'completely changed', 'switch', 'revolutionary'.

Answer d) can be classified as sameness with exception and difference. It uses a combination of the key words given in answers b) and c). If your answer is like this you like change but are also comfortable where things are evolving – evolution and revolution – but you don't really like sameness. You need major change every 3 years.

People who choose answers similar to c) and d) may not realise how much they want and need change. For instance, you may always find that you are buying the latest item of tack or clothing, or frequently changing instructors or livery yards, when what you need is a more radical change of direction and motivation. Maybe it is time to set a higher goal, or maybe significant change elsewhere in your life is required.

Believing you can ride better 4

The thing always happens that you really believe in; and the belief in a thing makes it happen. *Frank Lloyd Wright*

What do you believe?

'Whether you believe you can or can't…
you're right.'*

So now you know what you would love to have as **your goal**, and you understand more about **how you are motivated** and even **how to manage your expectations of success**. But …it still, somehow, just doesn't seem possible? Chances are you have some beliefs that are limiting you. **Beliefs determine** your expectations for yourself, others, your horses – in fact **every aspect of your life**. They can be spotted from the rules you make up and use in your everyday language.

The following phrases are all reflections of beliefs. 'Sitting trot is difficult'. 'You need a warmblood to win at dressage these days'. 'Only people with sponsors can afford to compete at national level.' They are initially created by 'reference experiences', the things you have seen, heard, read and felt that have determined what you think about any topic. However, they can become generalised over time and may lead to you holding very fixed ideas about certain subjects.

When you catch yourself using one of your beliefs, ask yourself 'Is it useful and does it serve me?' Notice which beliefs you already use that work for you and which ones it would be useful to change or have.

We tend to think of beliefs as all or nothing and that what we believe now will always be true. Yet a moment's thought and you will realise that many of your beliefs have changed through your life. You've let many of them go…such as Father Christmas…or perhaps that's one to keep!

case study

Case study: The impossible four-minute mile

Roger Bannister broke the four-minute mile on May 6 1954.

Before that day it was generally believed impossible to run a mile in such a short time. In the 10 years before, no one had even come close. Yet within 6 weeks another runner, the Australian John Landy, beat the new record by a second. Within 10 years nearly 200 people had broken that once impossible barrier. Once they believed it was possible, many more achieved it. Some stories say that Bannister was running to a false clock so he did not

consciously realise he had beaten the record until the official timekeepers told him the truth.

Roger Bannister repeatedly and intensely visualised breaking the four-minute barrier. We now realise this was like giving an unconscious command to his body.

* Henry Ford

Exercise 9:
Finding your riding beliefs

Complete the following phrases in your own words. Your answers will all be examples of your beliefs. Notice that some are more negative, or limiting, than others.

People with horses are ....

I am a ....rider.

When I have ridden well it is because...

When I ride badly it is because...

I'd ride better if I ....

Jumping is ....

Dressage is ....

Arab horses are ....

If I had more money I would ....

When I retire I will ....

The Success Cycle

'There is nothing either good or bad, but thinking makes it so.'*

Have you ever noticed how the **good riders always seem to be able to stay positive and brush off setbacks, while for the more negative riders things sometimes seem to go from bad to worse**, and they continually bemoan their lack of confidence, luck, whatever? Of course, it does seem as if all their bad luck and lack of success justifies their misery, but **their attitude can actually cause it**. The Success Cycle explains how. Identified by the East Germans in the 1970s, when their approach to sport was arguably the most effective in the world, it was subsequently developed into the AIMS (Acquiring Individual Mental Skills) system in Britain by Brian Miller, an international sports psychologist.

Who do you compare yourself to?

'If you compare yourself to God, you are going to look a little shabby...' Anon

If you find yourself making unflattering comparisons between yourself and someone else, consider how sensible your comparisons are. For instance, if you catch yourself saying 'Oh, I'm no good at jumping.' Ask 'No good at jumping compared to whom and at what standard?' If you are comparing yourself to your instructor or a professional competitor, is it surprising you are not as good as them when you haven't ridden as much or as many horses or jumped as many fences? The answer is no, of course.

This is a quick way to boost your confidence. Even if you are comparing yourself against other riders of a closer standard, remember to take into account aspects like how much time you have available to ride, how much experience you have, your horse's age and experience, and everything else you pack into your life!

At a simple level, if you believe you are a good rider (in comparison with your experience), you will be aware of all the best bits of your riding, and your confidence will be boosted. However, if you believe you are a bad or a nervous rider, you will magnify all the little mistakes out of all proportion. This is because you are focusing on what is going wrong. Therefore, a belief or attitude drives your behaviour and

determines your capability and performance: beliefs have a powerful self-fulfilling effect (see also pp.42–43).

A positive belief will lead to positive planning, happier thoughts and more proactive actions and, therefore, positive behaviour and performance. Where you choose to think more negatively, it can lead to more negative consequences, which will perpetuate your negative thoughts.

* William Shakespeare

The Success Cycle

POSITIVE BELIEF AND SELF IMAGE
I love going out for a hack on an autumn morning

POSITIVE ATTITUDE
I make sure we can be seen and that we are both relaxed and happy

POSITIVE EXPECTATION
I imagine having a lovely ride, seeing the beautiful autumn colours, hearing the birds, seeing my horse's breath like mist and feeling his springy steps

IMPROVED PERFORMANCE
I notice when I need to trot on ahead of traffic or turn into a passing place. I stay relaxed and calm

IMPROVED BEHAVIOURS
I can relax and yet still be aware of what is happening around us

NEGATIVE BELIEF AND SELF IMAGE
I'm scared of going for a hack

NEGATIVE ATTITUDE
I worry about hacking out, expecially on my own

NEGATIVE EXPECTATION
I notice how tense my horse is and can see all the spooky things coming up. I hear the cars as they approach us. I imagine an accident happening and all its consequences

DETERIORATING PERFORMANCE
I try not to get too nervous. I shorten the reins even though I know it makes my horse tense, and I end up gripping. I can't believe it when we get back home in one piece

LIMITING BEHAVIOUR
I put off going out so we are always in a hurry and flustered

Getting inside your beliefs

'The significant problems we face cannot be solved at the same level we were at when we created them.'*

We often **run our lives by a series of rules**, which operate at every level, from simple ideas to deeply held beliefs. They may come from school or a strong influence in our lives, such as a parent or grandparent. They are often supportive and make life easier: we never need to think or decide what to do, just follow them. However, **we can start to apply them in areas of our life where they are not as appropriate** and we don't realise when they hold us back. In the horse world there are many rules that come from the old systems of horse management and the cavalry, and they are much less relevant today. For example: You should always mount on the left (*otherwise your sword will get in the way*) and always water before feeding (*from the days when horses were watered from troughs – a horse with water continuously available will often drink during or after a feed*).

Exercise 10: Examining and evaluating your beliefs

Using the layout below as a template, list some of the beliefs or rules that you have in your life. Under the relevant headings, write down the age at which you first took it on as a rule or belief, who the rule came from or from what event, the benefits of the rule then, the benefits of the rule now, the disadvantages of the rule now. Examples are given to help you.

From this you can begin see that it is important to take time to think about what you say and begin to understand why you say it. Once you understand how or where your beliefs came in, it is easier to change them.

My rules and beliefs	Who did it come from?	Age when taken on	Benefits then	Benefits now	Disadvantages now
Those who ask don't get!	Mum	3–4	Gave Mum a quiet life! Stopped me having unreasonable expectations.	I don't have any high aspirations to try for.	Stops me goal setting. I think I don't deserve the things I want.
Don't stick your neck out. Keep your head down!	School	7	I wouldn't risk looking a fool. I kept quiet in class and never questioned the teacher.	I don't need to bother taking risks. I stay low profile!	I'm not used to looking good and winning.
Jumping is difficult.	Riding school teacher	16	It stopped her worrying about anyone falling off.	I'm not taking any risks.	I'll regret it if I don't get on and learn.

* *Albert Einstein*

Changing limiting beliefs

Recognising your limiting beliefs and making changes to them is one of the most effective ways you can make an impact on your performance. This is why it is useful to have an instructor or friend who will question you and point out when you are confident or doing something well. For shifting more deeply established limiting beliefs, it is helpful to consider impartial external help. The logical levels will also help you to get a deeper understanding of your beliefs and how they affect you, see pp.46–47.

Just a thought!

The bumble bee doesn't know it can't fly so it flies anyway.

Aerodynamically the bumble bee shouldn't be able to fly – its body is too heavy and its wings are too small and weak. Imagine what would happen if it knew what the scientists say!

Exercise 11: Confronting your limiting beliefs

Identify one of your limiting beliefs and then answer the questions below, writing your answers down. This will help you to understand how you took on the belief and what to replace it with. It's like a loosening up exercise to do before you go on to use other NLP belief-changing techniques.

My limiting belief is:

I can't afford to have a horse.

1 How long have I believed this for?

My parents always told me we couldn't afford one.

2 What or who gave me this limiting belief?

As a child my parents didn't really want me to ride, so they spent money on things like maths and music lessons and taking us on holiday abroad.

3 Given that situation, what was a good reason for that belief then?

Riding did cost a lot then, and there were my brother and sister to consider, too. My parents thought that holidays would be best for all the family.

4 Did I (or they) intend to limit myself in this way, forever?

Of course not! It was important to balance the needs of the whole family though.

5 What would I rather believe?

If I really want to own a horse and can balance it with my situation, now is the time to plan how to make it happen.

6 What will happen if I keep this belief?

I will think carefully about my situation and decide whether I am prepared to make the adjustments necessary to own a horse.

Questions for Karen

Karen, who we met earlier (see pp.16 and 32), discovered new things about herself from these questions. 'Before, I believed I couldn't afford more training. My new belief is that there are plenty of people I can help with their horses and that I can justify the training. As soon as I believed training was important to me, opportunities opened up to me, such as a government supported scheme towards my next exam. By asking myself the right questions and knowing what I wanted, I've got this sorted out!'

Exercise 12: Building a stronger belief

This exercise helps you to build a belief that you need in order to achieve a goal. The examples are provided to help you. Identify a belief about which you have some doubt. Write it down.

I can enjoy going for a gallop.

For each of the steps below, state this belief, follow it with the prompt words given and then complete each sentence with whatever comes to mind once you have read the question.

Because I … (Why is it desirable or appropriate? Are you capable of reaching the outcome?)
I can enjoy going for a gallop because then I will know I have reached a better standard of riding.

After I … (What has to happen to support this belief?)
I can enjoy going for a gallop after I have developed my confidence and trust in my horse.

While I … (What else is going on concurrently with this belief?)
I can enjoy going for a gallop while I take lessons to improve my position.

Whenever I … (What is a key condition relating to this belief?)
I can enjoy going for a gallop whenever I know I can stay in control of my horse if he has a spook or a buck.

So that I … (What is the intention of this belief?)
I can enjoy going for a gallop so that I will be able to go for long rides out in the country.

If I … (What constraints or results relate to this belief?)
I can enjoy going for a gallop, if I feel the ground and weather is appropriate to do so.

In the same way that I … (What is a similar belief that you already have?)
I can enjoy going for a gallop in the same way that I enjoy driving my car.

Read all your answers together and notice what has changed or become clearer to you about achieving this belief or goal. Put all of the findings together to create a paragraph that is a coherent set of ideas and affirmations and use this to strengthen your confidence in the belief.

The example above could read: *I can enjoy going for a gallop if I feel the ground and weather are appropriate to do so and after I have developed my confidence and trust through taking lessons to improve my position. I will have reached a better standard of riding and be more confident, knowing that I can stay in control of my horse if he has a spook or a buck. Then I will be able to go for long distance rides – it will be just like driving my car wherever I want, at the speed I want…*

Understanding your riding inspiration 5

In horsemanship, the vehicle of enlightenment is the horse, and the horse is nature itself... Since the horse is nature itself, the lessons are incredibly profound. The moment the horseman/rider succumbs to the lessons of the horse, they have transcended the duality of man and nature, man against nature. *Paul Belasik*

Thinking riding

'We are what we think. All that we are arises with our thoughts.

With our thoughts, we make our world.'*

Think about the most **inspired people** you have heard about – Ghandi, Martin Luther King, Mother Theresa. Such people often **have a spiritual calling or mission** that drives them to work towards their vision. Paul Belasik has done much to open the discussion of the **spirituality of the horse/rider relationship** in his books.

The logical levels is a concept that helps to show the relationship between different aspects of our personality and our lives by linking our choices and our behaviour and beliefs. For you to achieve your dreams and to experience inner harmony, each logical level has to be in alignment with that above and below it. Where there is a lack of alignment, there will be incongruence (a feeling that your words and behaviour don't match up), which may lead to uncertainty or confusion.

Use the triangle, which was originally devised by NLP co-developer Robert Dilts, to explore your relationship with horses and riding.

The highest logical level is our spirituality and mission. Beneath this is identity, which drives our beliefs and values. These in turn drive the skills and capabilities that we allow ourselves to demonstrate. The concepts towards the bottom of the triangle are practical and fairly basic: our behaviour and the environment we operate in.

SPIRITUALITY & MISSION:
What is my relationship with horses?

IDENTITY:
Who am I when I ride?

BELIEFS AND VALUES:
Why do I love riding so much?

SKILLS & CAPABILITIES:
How can I ride better?

BEHAVIOUR:
What do I do to get canter?

ENVIRONMENT:
Where shall I ride, what shall I wear?

* Buddha

Interpreting the logical levels triangle

Environment, behaviour and skills

Look at the logical levels triangle from a horse-riding perspective. A 'good' rider is naturally aligned at all levels. For instance, controlling your horse can start with consideration of the tack you ride him in – bits, noseband, martingales. These are environmental issues. How you use these artificial aids is a behaviour – do your hands move, do you keep a tight grip on the reins? Then consider how soft your contact can be and how easily your body follows the movement of your horse to allow him to take the bit and work in an outline – this is a skill or capability – and it is the level where good and bad habits operate.

Beliefs

Many worries in riding are centered around beliefs, often ones that may be inappropriate. For example, what do you believe about controlling horses? Many people believe they are irrational or flighty, or even naughty. This is not the case: horses are prey animals; their sensory systems are equipped accordingly, and so they behave in appropriate patterns. Do you worry about whether your horse will spook or bolt with you? What would it be like to believe that you can handle your horse, even in conditions where he might spook?

Identity and spirituality

Next is the identity level. Top riders will say, for example, 'I am a showjumper' or 'I am a dressage rider' – these are identity level statements. By being precise about who they are they have a clear vision of what that means in terms of the beliefs, the skills and the behaviours that subsequently go with it. By having such a clear and precise identity they are thus able to harness the appropriate emotional state they need for a particular situation: relaxed and calm, or determined and focused, for example.

At spiritual or mission level, people often speak of having a high regard for the horse, or a love of connecting with nature through the horse. If this is your highest reason for riding, is it wholly reflected in the way you ride, the tack you use, the way you respond in difficult situations and the beliefs you have?

Aligning the levels

From this you can see how being a good rider is about being one at every level: from the tack you use or the way you sit, to what you believe and who you consider you are when you ride. Imagine a horse that can be strong when ridden. An inexperienced rider will simply make adjustments at the environmental level – using a stronger bit – whereas a better rider would invest in schooling time or continuing to ride the horse with the belief that it just needs to learn to slow down. A better rider would also consider why the horse is behaving this way and would check out possible physical and emotional factors, such as teeth, tack fitting, stable management and pain, as causes of resistance, instead of just going for a stronger bit.

Core beliefs about identity are often at the heart of your personality and they have the greatest impact on your behaviour and experience. They are usually laid down very early in life. Useful beliefs give an empowering permission and motivation to use your skills to the full. When you change a belief, you will also change a lot of behaviour. However, when you try to change your behaviour, it is unlikely to stick if it conflicts with a strongly held belief.

Operating levels

When you come across a statement that shows you have misalignment in your logical levels, it is helpful to identify at what level the statement operates, and then to work with it at that level.

For instance:
- 'I don't want to jump that jump' is about **behaviour** – and not doing something.
- 'I can't jump that high' is about **capability** – whether you can or can't do something.
- 'I'll never jump that high' is a **belief**.
- 'I'm not a show jumper' is about **identity**.

The value of values

'...the act and art of riding is in itself the reward, the path to **enlightenment, education, self development...'***

By understanding what your core values are, you can use them to **make decisions you will be happy with** (see also logical levels, pp.46–47). Think about someone who takes a stand for what they really believe in. They will have consistent themes – values – that guide their actions. **What could you accomplish if you focused only on what was important to you in your riding life?**

* Paul Belasik

Exercise 13: Identifying your core values

1 Decide on an activity that you enjoy, such as jumping, hacking out or competing. Get a friend to write this at the bottom of a piece of paper. You answers will gradually build into a chart like the example below.

2 Now your friend either asks 'Why is … important to you?' or 'What does … give you?' It's important that these exact questions are used because they produce certain responses. Other similar-seeming questions, such as 'Why do you enjoy that?', would find out about something different. You may have several reasons, each of which your friend should write down above where your enjoyable activity is written.

3 Taking each of these reasons, your friend asks one of the same original questions. 'Why is … important to you?' or 'What does that give you?'

4 Work methodically through every statement until you feel you cannot answer any more, or the same answer comes up. The process is like unpeeling an onion. There will begin to be some repetition as your core values emerge.

Look at the example chart and the one that you and your friend have created and notice how the themes emerge, develop and interlink. Try repeating this exercise for other areas or interests in your life and you will find that they share common themes. For instance, in the example given relationship with nature may be reflected at home with a desire not to use pesticides or eating vegetarian food.

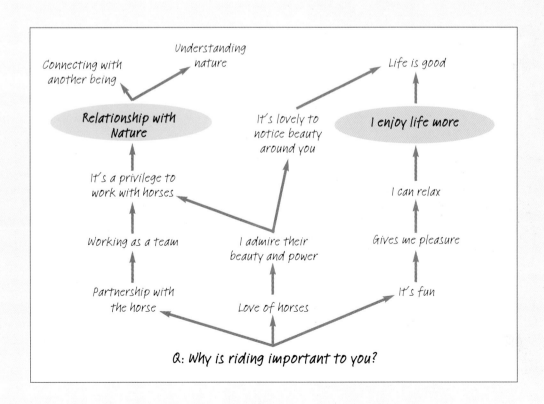

Exercise 14: Finding your weakest link!

Using the logical levels can help you improve your performance. Think about a problem – or a limiting belief – you have with your riding and want to change. For instance, it could be that you want to improve your confidence when jumping or accuracy when riding a dressage test or calmness when handling young lively horses.

As you think about yourself in the problem situation, work through the following questions, writing your answers down. An example is given to help you. It is about improving the score in a dressage test. Work through the questions and you will see that performance is blocked at one or two points, in this case behaviour (2) and capability (3).

1 Where am I? What are the surroundings like in the situation I'm considering?

At an affiliated dressage show with lots of glamorous looking horses and riders working in around me.

2 How am I behaving in this situation?

I am beginning to feel intimidated and wonder whether I should be here at all. This makes me worried and nervous and my horse becomes tense and restricted, too.

3 What are the capabilities and skills I have or need to have?

I know I can ride softly, calmly and accurately at home.

4 Why am I doing this, and why?

I enjoy getting out and competing and like to measure our progress through our performance, because I also enjoy learning and developing, especially through the horse. It is also my way to get away from the stresses of work and life in general.

5 Who am I when I behave like this?

I am open to constructive feedback, putting in place what I have learnt – I am someone who deserves to be placed at this level. I can be a winner!

6 How do I relate to others when I am like this?

I can be relaxed and friendly yet professional and calm as I work in and perform a polished, accurate test.

Case study: Logical levels in action

Margaret had always had horses. She was a great animal lover and very committed to her animals. At the age of 40 she bought a ¾ Thoroughbred, Monty, to be her competition horse, to start dressage and show jumping with.

Monty was very different from the 20-year-old mare Margaret was starting to retire. However, Margaret knew that she would need to learn new approaches and improve her riding, and so she started out on lessons. Monty was, indeed, a handful and Margaret had a number of falls, and then, when she'd had him nine months, she ended up in hospital with bad concussion after a fall at a jumping clinic.

Nine years later Margaret came to me. She had assumed she would get over these memories, but in fact they were getting worse and she was now imagining many new horrors, too! **Over the years she had been getting more and more anxious about riding and she realised that she was not enjoying Monty** as much as she would have liked. They had a working relationship, but she wanted to really be happy riding him and feel confident about him.

When we worked together I used a combination of techniques to clear the old memories, however, it was the logical levels exercise that gave Margaret the tools to go out and rework her relationship with Monty.

Margaret's hierarchy

Spiritual	Relationship with all living things.
Identity	I can learn about relationships, I am adaptable.
Beliefs	Different needs need different responses.
Capability	Recognising the horse's needs, enjoying the process of adapting to them.
Behaviour	Listening and asking questions, thoughtful about the behaviour of both horses and people.
Environment	At the yard with the horses and owners.

Having identified Margaret's logical levels, we wrote each one on a piece of paper and placed them in a line on the floor, a step apart. This gave each a 'spatial anchor' with all the feelings and images that were relevant to it. We started at the top of the hierarchy, with the spiritual feeling of being connected and having a relationship with all living things. I anchored this feeling with a touch, then asked Margaret to think about the problems she was having. As she stepped through each of the levels, Margaret realised that she was behaving out of alignment with her identity and her beliefs and values. **Because she was behaving contrary to what she believed, she was tense and nervous.**

She stepped off the pieces of paper and I activated the anchor of the spiritual feeling by touching it. Then we started at the lower end of the hierarchy, recreating the environment space. Margaret realised that there were some negative people in the yard who spoke of doom and gloom a lot, something that was in opposition to her naturally positive and loving outlook. She decided she could reduce the time she spent with these people. In the behaviour space, she realised that it would be helpful to have someone watching her ride so that she could bounce her thoughts off them – her husband and friends would be happy to help. That process would help her be aware of her riding and how she was responding to Monty. She could see herself more relaxed and thinking about her position more.

see also:
The Phobia Cure p.134
Re-imprinting p.138
Anchors p.86

Carrying her beliefs forward to her capabilities when riding Monty, Margaret realised that she could think more about life from his point of view, including the things that caused him to spook or tense up. From this perspective she would be able to respond more quickly and appropriately.

A horse is simply a horse

Sometimes, rather than change, some people blame their horse. Do you say that Todd is scared of cows or that Luca can only jump 2ft 6in, that Pebbles is too old to learn to go on the bit, or that Oscar always bucks when we canter? If so, ask yourself whether another more experienced or confident rider would have the same problem? If yes, then perhaps that horse isn't for you. But remember it is unfair to blame the horse when the issue lies with your confidence, ability, weight, fitness or whatever. After all these are all things you can work on – the horse is simply being a horse and responding to you as you are at the moment.

'There is no failure only feedback'

Keeping a setback in perspective, and looking for the learning in it – the thing you will do differently next time – is an extremely useful skill to develop. Don't take a mistake personally, at identity level, but instead look at your skills, capabilities and behaviours – you can find a way to create a positive out of the negative. Even when I am working with people who have experienced major setbacks – from crashing falls to road accidents – I notice that they can start to list what they have learnt and what they would do differently next time. The changes they would make are at every level: one rider realised she had let herself be completely over-horsed by boasting that she was much more experienced (capability) than she was, another that when jumping she needed to sit up and hold the horse to the fence instead of letting him go on a long stride (behaviour).

Starting to look at situations from a fresh perspective is an important part of several NLP change processes that are discussed later, especially exercise 35, The Phobia Cure (p.134). The skill is also looked at in Ask a better question (p.62–63) and Take a different perspective (p.96).

Tips for managing progress

- Be aware of your self-talk, see p.54.
- Remind yourself of the areas in your skills and knowledge where you are confident.
- Choose friends and instructors who will reflect your strengths back to you to help you through the downs, see p.126.
- At plateau or relapse points, see exercises 16 and 34 (pp.62 and 131) on reframing.
- For identity threshold challenges, read about re-imprinting, p.138.

Talking yourself into riding well 6

Success is as much a limitation to creativity as failure. Robert Dilts

The power of your words

'The meaning of your communication is the response you get…which may be different from the one you intended.'*

What you say about yourself and to yourself **are your beliefs**, and your unconscious mind looks for **reinforcement** and **justification** of them. Think about what happens when you say 'I'm a nervous rider' or 'I always forget my test'. What about 'I love going for a gallop', 'I'm going to ride a really accurate test'? Notice how much more positive these statements sound, and imagine the feelings and images they create when you can say them with conviction.

Because we've been able to speak for years, we talk fluently now; we choose our words without having to think about sentence structure or how to place emphasis. Our use of language is driven not only by learning but also by our beliefs and values (see pp.42 and 48). Therefore, when we communicate with others, we interact with their beliefs. We also respond to one another's language and, consequently, modify our own: it is impossible to be without influence or to be uninfluenced by others. Start listening to your own language and that of other people. Look for the beliefs and presuppositions behind the words.

Case study: Breaking negative thought patterns

At one college lecture one of the students, John, said 'this is all very well, but what about reality?'

He continued: 'It costs a lot of money to compete at eventing, you have to have a string of horses and the best two could both go lame just before the big event you have trained and trained for. **I can't see how this goal setting works, in the end it's all down to luck and having the money to keep covering for things going wrong**…' His is a common cry, so it is useful to consider the points that he, and so many others have made.

The results may surprise you. The success cycle shows that John's comments are simply a combination of negative thinking and limiting beliefs. For instance, 'it costs a lot of money', 'you have to have a string of horses', 'it's all down to luck' and 'things will always go wrong' all reflect limiting beliefs. Top riders, including Reiner Klimke, the Schockemöhles and Pierre Durrand, have had to arrange their business careers so that they could ride, and many other riders have got to where they are by working very hard in a good yard, ready to take any opportunity to learn and prove themselves.

It is very important to notice such patterns of thought, and to be able to analyse your limiting beliefs and think about alternative, more empowering ones.

see also:
The Success Cycle
p.40

* NLP Presupposition

Filters

We do not operate directly on the world, we create maps from our sensory experience, then operate from our maps. However the map is not the territory. And it is much easier to change the map than the territory.

NLP Presupposition

We use our past experiences to help us to find our way through our world. Each time we have a new experience, we use 'filters' to match it with a previous experience and then know how to respond. Filters belong to one of the following categories: generalisation, deletion, distortion, presupposition (see pp.56–57). For example, filters are the reason why someone can say with such conviction (generalise) that they don't like chestnut mares or that they are scared of jumping. What has happened is that one or two key experiences have defined 'chestnut mares' or 'jumping' for them. These experiences may well have been unpleasant, but it doesn't mean that forever after that is always going to be the case, and so be the 'truth'. However, the more we look for proof that chestnut mares are not as good as geldings or that jumping is too risky, or whatever, the more we will find that proof. We do this by not noticing (deleting) the nice or talented chestnut mares we have met or forgetting (deleting) all the times when a gelding we know behaves in the same way. We misunderstand (distort)

Telling the truth

If you ask several people to complete the phrase 'Jumping is...', one person might say 'It's scary and difficult', another 'It's easy, the best thing ever, a fantastic liberating experience' and someone else 'It's just for confident riders'. Each reply is correct because it is based on that person's experience of jumping, even if they have never jumped and it is just what they have heard other people saying about jumping. What a person says tells us what they believe about a subject.

the big smiles someone has when they jump a round, seeing these smiles only as relief that the person didn't fall off, and we choose to ignore the fact that 99.99 percent of the time no one gets hurt, even if falls do occur. By presupposing that the competition will be too intense or the jumps too big, we may stop ourselves from even entering or going to a show.

When people have an open mind or where they know they are still learning, such deletions, distortions and generalisations get caught and reconsidered and put in a wider context. However, as we become more

established in our worlds, it becomes easy to make these statements so that we don't have to continually adjust to the new ideas we are experiencing. This is particularly the case with 'experts' or those in authority who can feel threatened at having to alter their beliefs in the light of new experiences – they can become dogmatic and entrenched. For this reason, I prefer to have an instructor who is still learning and being taught themselves!

How can we use all this knowledge to achieve better and more powerful communication? One way is to identify the filters people are using, then we can ask better questions, to see how their map of the world is structured, and indeed to catch our own assumptions. It is surprising just how unaware of our own statements we can be – often they prove to be unconsidered.

Filter

Generalisation

With generalisations, elements of your world become separated from their original context and are used to represent a whole range of situations. Once adopted, a generalisation may distort an experience to make it consistent with your expectations. For instance, when you first start riding, the statement 'one end of a horse kicks and the other bites' is a very useful warning, but it won't give you confidence long-term. Likewise, 'You shouldn't hope to win' might be well intentioned when you first start competing but it is not helpful when you have invested time and money in your training and have qualified for the championships. Unless you look for experiences to negate this type of generalisation, or accept external challenges to them, your expectations will be confirmed and the cycle will be repeated.

Distortion

Distortion can be a useful filter, which allows us to make alterations in our experiences in order to have dreams and fantasy. Distortion is fine if it empowers you with a dream, otherwise check out your approach to 'reality – you may find yourself imagining things that simply aren't there.

Examples

Watch out for **'always'**, **'never'**, **'nobody'**, **' everybody'**, **'all'**, **'every'** – they always signal a generalisation.

'I always forget my dressage test.' The chances are that you are ignoring the 99 percent of times when you do OK. You don't get forget every single movement do you? Think about how to state the situation more truthfully. It may be that you are worried about forgetting the order of the movements or that you remember how flustered you became when you once forgot. Catch and stop this type of comment, otherwise it may expand: **'I can't jump'** soon becomes **'I can't jump, canter in big fields or go to shows.'**

When you notice generalisations, ask questions like **'Why not just have a short canter towards the gate?'** or **'How do other people manage it?'** or **'What will happen if you do it in a sensible planned way?'**

Do you say things like **'I must clean my tack daily'**, **'I should be able to jump that jump'**, **'I ought to muck out before I ride'**. Ask **'Who says?'** or **'Why?'** Musts, shoulds and oughts can often be traced back to parents and teachers. They may link back to little beliefs or rules we take for granted. Maybe they are less relevant now – so think what would happen if you bent them a little.

Some people say these words kick them into action. But consider these two sets of phrases. **'You should do this'**, **'You must practise more'**, **'You ought to work harder'**. And: **'I choose to do this'**, **'I will practise more'**, **'I can work harder'**. Say them aloud to yourself and notice the difference in your motivation. In the second set you have given yourself choice.

'I'm sure he meant to hurt me when he bucked me off' is a mind read. You cannot possibly know what your horse intended.

'It's selfish to want to win' is a lost performative. The criterion for the judgement is lost: who says it is selfish to want to win?

'My boyfriend never cleans my tack, that means he hates my horses' is an extreme example of what is called the 'cause-effect' distortion. In this, a link is implied that is simply not there.

Words like **'don't'** or **'can't'** make the recipient think of doing what they are told not to first. For example, **'don't lift your hands'**, **'don't grip with your knees'**, **'don't forget your gloves'**… In order to 'obey' you have to put your attention on the 'wrong' thing.

Filter	Examples

Deletion

This is where we pay attention only to certain parts of our experiences, excluding other things that have happened. Deletion reduces the world to proportions we feel capable of handling, which is sometimes useful, sometimes not.

All around you people are speaking in deletions: be aware of it so that you don't end up agreeing with what they are saying when you don't know what it is they actually mean!

'I'm always nervous'. By saying this, you have deleted what you are nervous about, along with all the times when you weren't nervous. To challenge such deletions you could respond **'Nervous about what specifically?'** or **'How do you know you are nervous?'** **'Sitting trot is bad for me.'** Find out how it's bad, by asking **'In what way?'**

'Jumping is dangerous' or **'Dressage is boring'**. Ask **'How is it dangerous?'** and **'Why is it boring?'** Remember, it's the speaker's filter that it is most useful to be aware of because it gives us a chance to find out more about their attitude, not their actual words and opinions.

'She's a better rider' is a comparative deletion. The person that 'she' is being compared to is missed out. Ask **'Better than whom?'** or **'In what circumstances is she a better rider?'**
Comparative deletions are often used in advertising: **'Horses prefer X feed.'** Ask **'Which horses prefer X feed to which other feeds?'**

Presupposition

Our 'world map' contains some presuppositions. Words like car or saddle or horse all induce us to make presuppositions. Too many or too emphatic presuppositions about things that are in reality variable – chestnut mares, for example – may prevent us from recognising the benefits of other views of the world.

Presuppositions are found throughout our language and can be used to imply behaviour and reactions.
'Do you want to jump this fence on the left or right rein?' The instructor has presupposed that the rider will jump the fence.

The word **'saddle'** presupposes a set of relationships – something to ride a horse with, stirrups, seat, cantle, pommel – however, it doesn't necessarily presuppose what the saddle is made of, what style it is, what size it is, and so on. These are all variables within the term 'saddle'.

We have presuppositions about the attributes of breeds of horses or their sex – just listen to some people talk about **Arab horses** or **chestnut mares** – and maybe about the characteristics of categories of people.

Exercise 15:
Identifying filters

Can you identify the generalisation, deletion, distortion or presupposition in the following phrases? How would you reply to them to counter them?

Statement	Filter	How do you reply?
Everybody else can afford to go to shows and have lessons.	Generalisation	*Everybody?!! What do you have to do differently to be able to afford to go?*
I've got to ride him.		
I want to know I'm good enough to handle him		
I need to work on everything I am not good at.		
Having more horses will open up new opportunities for me.		
I would love to compete again and meet old friends.		
I would like to feel I could go for a gallop without falling off.		
We have horses so we can't go on holiday.		
You shouldn't mount from the right.		
He's doing poorly at Novice – He'll never make Elementary.		

Change what you say about your riding 7

My life has been filled with terrible misfortune, most of which never happened. *Montaigne*

Use positive language

'Habit is either the best of servants…
or the worst of masters.'*

To start improving and changing your beliefs, you need to **listen to the words you use when you talk about yourself.** Think about what they actually say. **Ask better questions!** When you ask 'How can I start to enjoy jumping?' you will get a completely different set of answers to those you'd get if you asked 'Why am I scared of jumping?' The same goes for the questions others ask us. If your instructor asks 'Why can't you ride that turn like I told you?', you will come up with all the reasons why you can't. Imagine the difference in your answer if, instead, the instructor had asked 'How can you improve that turn?'

Stop hoping or trying

Erase 'hope to' and 'try to' from your language. By now you should be aware that hoping for something is not enough (see goal setting pp.20–23).

What are you going to do to help get what you want? Be more positive and less passive. For example, instead of saying 'I hope I will remember the course', say 'I'll remember the course'. Instead of 'I'll try to jump the fence', say 'I will jump the fence'.

These alternatives act like a command to your unconscious mind, it's something you *will* do. To say I hope or I'll try indicates that it doesn't matter if you do or you don't, it's very passive. Be clear, positive and active about what you want.

And don't do that!

How commands are phrased is equally important. For instance, if your instructor says to you 'Don't lift up your hands, you first have to imagine lifting your hands then you have to mentally delete or 'cross out' the order (see p.57). Meanwhile your mind works so fast that the chances are you will have lifted your hands anyway.

Instead the instructor could say something like 'Think about where your hands should be' or 'How can you improve the contact?' It's a very simple difference, but it works.

Positive intent

Imagine that all behaviour has a positive intention. Once you know what that positive intention is, it gives you an understanding of how to change the behaviour. For instance, the positive intention behind aggression is often self-protection or fear.

Notice how often we tell ourselves that we're not capable or good enough, or have other self-critical thoughts. By thinking about the positive intention of your internal voice, you can often understand its roots. Consider this statement: 'It's dangerous to jump.' Ask yourself what is the positive intention for saying that. The statement might then become 'You need to look after yourself.' Ask what is the positive intention of the second statement. It might then become 'I want to protect you by making you scared of jumping.'

Once you know that your 'inner voice' is trying to protect you, you can think of other ways of reassuring it. As a concept, positive intention is very valuable in relating to your horse, especially as it won't have as many hidden agendas and learned behaviours as a person. For example, if your horse is playing spook and you decide it is simply youthful energy and freshness, you will respond differently than if the spooking was an evasion due to stiffness or lack of confidence.

*Nathaniel Emmons

If it's not your fault, whose is it?

Sometimes people come to a situation with ready-made excuses for performing badly:

- `'I'm not well-prepared.'`
- `'I think I may be getting flu.'`
- `'I've had no time to practise or warm up my horse.'`
- `'I haven't learned the test properly.'`

Note such excuses, especially if you make them all the time. Could you assume more responsibility for your preparation, arrival time, abilities – even the state of your health? If you think other people are always to blame, remember you are part of the relationship. And you could consider whether it would be better to pull out of an event if you are not prepared sufficiently.

Timescales

The effect of timescale in language is also very powerful. Say these sentences and notice about the feeling you get from each:

- `'I have jumped a 1.10m course.'`
- `'I am jumping 1.10m courses.'`
- `'I will be jumping 1.10m courses.'`

By paying attention to the implied timescales in your language, you can build possibility into a situation. Suppose you often say 'I'm disorganised'. This implies that your disorganisation is unchangeable, and is rooted in the past. Instead say 'I want to be more organised'. This implies all the time, and that there is a future with organised behaviour in it. It makes you start to think of how you can become organised.

Moving from negative to positive

You may say 'These are only words; I don't really mean it.' But you do mean it! Your unconscious is selecting the words (see p.54). Think how much better it is to say more positive things to yourself than just letting habitually negative words undermine your self image. Talking about what you are doing less well simply draws attention to it. Affirmations (p.25) and being positive about what you say to yourself can be effective: even if you currently don't enjoy jumping or galloping, or whatever, if you want to feel better about it, add words like 'I'm going to learn how to be more confident...' Correct your negative comments immediately – revise your thoughts and say them out loud, too. In time, you can nip the negative thought before it is even thought!

Consider these examples of swapping negative language over to more positive comments.

'I don't have a problem with that.'	`'That is a good idea.'`
'I don't think I can jump that.'	`'I'll jump it when I feel confident enough.'`
'Don't be tense – don't slouch.'	`'Sit tall in the saddle – relax, head up.'`
'It wasn't too bad.'	`'Some of that was very good.'`
'I can't see what else I can do.'	`'We need to think of some more ideas.'`
'I'm sure that won't work.'	`'What can I do to help make it work?'`
'I'm useless.'	`'What am I doing well?'`
'That's not too bad for a beginner.'	`'Well done!'`
'He won't let me pick up his foot.'	`'How can I pick his foot up?'`
'I'm sure to fall off.'	`'I can ride securely.'`
'Don't forget your gloves.'	`'Remember your gloves.'`

Warning! When you hear others talk in negatives, try not to plunge in and correct them, unless you are sure you have good rapport with them. Sometimes if you're too enthusiastic about positive thinking others become negative – about you.

Ask a better question

Life is a series of ups…
and downs

The way you **understand an event is influenced by your perspective**: this is called the frame in NLP. **Reframing is used** to change the frame **to alter the event's meaning**, which will almost inevitably change your responses and behaviours. Reframing is useful in cases where beliefs are so ingrained that they are hard to move on just with self-talk.

Exercise 16: Questions to change your thinking

The reframing exercise helps you to re-orientate your thinking. Look at the diagram and you will see how different responses can be made to the original statement to help someone re-orientate their thinking. These may be made as quick comments or you can work out an answer under each category. Whichever way you use reframing, avoid being drawn into discussion: work through all the responses first. Their cumulative effect will change the way you think about the issue. It works like a drip of water wearing away stone, loosening up the thinking that has held the belief in place.

1 Look at the diagram and the sample responses to the statement. The bold titles explain the different frames.
2 Now make up your own responses to your own statement. This takes a little practice but it is a useful skill to have in all sorts of situations.
3 To build on this exercise, list all the things you learnt from the different responses, and then the benefits of challenging your original statement. This might seem a bit odd, but often a person will realise that after just one event, they started to behave differently. Usually, that dramatic event was like a big lesson so when they look back they can see that it was here that it all started to go wrong and, therefore, they can see a way to change their behaviour.

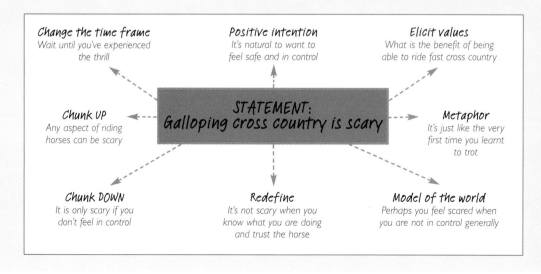

Change the time frame
Wait until you've experienced the thrill

Positive intention
It's natural to want to feel safe and in control

Elicit values
What is the benefit of being able to ride fast cross country

Chunk UP
Any aspect of riding horses can be scary

STATEMENT:
Galloping cross country is scary

Metaphor
It's just like the very first time you learnt to trot

Chunk DOWN
It is only scary if you don't feel in control

Redefine
It's not scary when you know what you are doing and trust the horse

Model of the world
Perhaps you feel scared when you are not in control generally

Case study: Reframing Frances

Can you recognise this scenario: leaving for the show a little late, a hold-up on the way, getting there and realising that the event was bigger than we had thought and there are people who we want to go well in front of? When he is unloaded, our horse picks up the atmosphere and our tension, and it's a little bit windy as well, just for good measure. Then we find out that the class is running a little early – hurry!

All this happened to Frances and resulted in her horse spooking in the warm-up and taking-off through the showground, slipping and falling, and receiving a nasty cut. After the fall, she found that she increasingly lost her nerve about competing and would make all sorts of excuses not to go.

In the reframing exercise we took the phrase 'I don't like going to shows anymore', and she found that the questions that really provoked her were:

- *What was important to you about going to shows?* (eliciting values)
- *What else do you not like doing anymore?* (chunk up).
- *Why did you enjoy going to shows before?* (change time frame)
- *Would you rather hide your horse away like a hermit?* (metaphor)

and finally

- *What would your horse prefer?* (redefine)

In our session, we also worked through anchoring to give Frances an extra resource, and looked at the episode from different perceptual positions, ie from the perspective of an impartial observer and from the horse's point of view. Then we finished by reviewing the lessons learnt from the episode, which is another form of reframing.

Here is the list Frances came up with:

1 *I need to get to the show with plenty of time in hand and have a proper warm-up.*

2 *I need to work my horse the day before since he tends to spook more when he is fresh.*

3 *I had a dramatic experience from which we both walked away unhurt – and it's made me think more about why I am riding.*

4 *I set myself up for not doing well by always being a bit late.*

5 *If I get really delayed I can ask the organiser to change my time, or even just ride at the show and don't compete – it's all good experience anyway.*

6 *Now I know how to keep calm and remember that I am riding for pleasure*

7 *I do want to get on and compete.*

Once you can talk about the benefits and what you learnt from having had an accident, it is surprising how easy it is to see it as not such a big deal, especially since you also know now what you would do differently next time.

> see also:
> Anchoring p.86
> Perceptual Positions p.96

With significant incidents, perhaps where a horse or rider was injured, I would use additional NLP techniques to help. A one-to-one session with a fully qualified Master Practitioner could also be appropriate.

Is your horse a gentle giant?

'The real voyage of discovery consists not in seeking new landscapes but in having new eyes.'*

Like individual words, **metaphors also have an impact on how we think**. For instance, you may say the horse is 'a gentle giant' or that he is 'as soft as butter', instead of simply that he was very kind or calm. **A metaphor often has more impact than an individual word** to both the listener and the person stating it. It reflects the feeling the speaker really has about something, even though the meaning of the words is not actually 'true'. Metaphorical stories are a highly effective way to allow the unconscious mind to reach its own conclusions.

Metaphors can be stories, phrases, colloquial expressions or just words (often linked to VAK language, see p.71). When you notice them as part of conversation you can use them by asking questions to enhance or loosen them up.

Consider the following examples:

- Is something **holding you back** from your goal**?**
- Can you **float above** the detail**?**
- Ride the course in a really **bold attacking way!**

What is it like to ride your horse?

If I ask you 'What is it like to ride your horse?', I am asking for a metaphor. Suppose you replied 'It is like a beautiful dance, we are two partners moving in harmony.' You would be starting a metaphor, that of dancing. It is then very easy to continue the conversation using other ideas from that metaphor and developing it further by talking about what music you are playing. Another example would be to reply: 'It's like driving a finely tuned performance car…'. And this could be developed by describing the road you are on and where it is taking you. Positive metaphors provide a wealth of mutual experiences to build upon, and it can be fun conversing in them.

However, suppose you were to answer that it is 'a never-ending battle' or 'like being blindfold on a rollercoaster, not knowing what is going to happen next.' These are two very different experiences, and not necessarily positive! For the first, I would want to ask what the battle was about and how you could make peace. For the second, I would want to know whether you enjoyed theme park rides or why you chose to take them, then what it would be like if you took off the blindfold. In the second instance, the reply could be that you enjoy looking back on a

Know your mind

Metaphors are a graphic form of unconscious communication. By noticing them and thinking about them, you are accessing your unconscious mind. This is the source of your dreams and your fears, so the more you learn how to access it and adapt it, the more you are using your greatest resource. When you reflect other people's metaphors back to them, you will build an unconscious connection between you and this helps your rapport. Start listening out for all the metaphors around you.

* Marcel Proust

'difficult' ride but are finding the stress of riding through it is now too much. You might realise that you didn't know you'd put a 'blindfold' on until your innocent comment was challenged. And, if you didn't realise you had a blindfold, then the chances are that you hadn't thought of taking it off! Now imagine riding without the blindfold, and preparing for all the ups and downs by being fully aware of what is happening around you. It wouldn't be so dramatic,

nor so stressful. In the long run you may need to understand why you look for drama and whether this pattern repeats itself in other areas of your life, too.

From this you can see that even negative metaphors can provide a valuable way of understanding your motivation and deeper feelings about something. Just conversing at this level will provide insights and can even start to make changes in your attitudes and then your beliefs.

Exercise 17: Using metaphors

To help you with this exercise, imagine using a metaphor about your horse growing up so you think in terms of 'well we've only just backed this one, he's a little green, he has learnt plenty already'. Or consider the seasons 'maybe this is still winter – but spring is on the way!' Whenever you work with long-term metaphors such as these, there is a certain inevitability that things will change, and this prevents you getting stuck in the generalisation 'never' (see p.56).

Think of ways to remind yourself about your positive metaphors, things that can be tangible or visual – anything that reminds you of the metaphor. For the examples discussed on these pages it could be a picture of dancers, a little model of a sports car, a postcard from a fairground.

1 Think about the metaphors you use to describe your riding or your relationship with your horse

2 Write them down in full and look at them.

3 How do they make you feel,

4 How could you change or develop your metaphors?

Exercise 18:
Simple belief changes

You can loosen up and start to change a belief by working through the following steps, which use the ideas of positive language. Take a typical statement you often make about yourself and your riding, and follow the steps, writing down each phrase in full each time.

1   Write down your limiting belief.   *I can't ride.*

2   Write down its linguistic opposite.   *I can ride well.*

3   Add a process into the sentence, such as start to, learn, realise, notice. This puts the activity into the present and future.   *I could learn to ride well.*

4   Add a word with some motivation and pleasure behind it (an empowering word), such as enjoy, effective, easy. This helps you to realise the steps you will take.   *It would be so rewarding to learn to ride really well.*

Compare the starting belief to this new one. Can you believe it? Does it feel better? Think about how it will be to have this new belief in the future.

Improving your riding through your senses

A man's mind, stretched by a new idea, can never go back to its original dimension. Anon

Making sense of your memories

Everything you have ever experienced has been absorbed by your senses.

There are five senses, or sensory modes – **seeing, hearing, touch, smell and taste**, which can take in thousands of pieces of information in a moment. **Your unconscious mind will notice and monitor them** – seeing the flick of horse's ear, feeling its heart rate, hearing birds in the distance, and so on – but only a very few (about seven) will be brought to your conscious attention at any one time, because they are completely irrelevant to what you are doing and thinking at the time.

While our unconscious is filtering all this information and our body is responding to the messages sent by the brain, our conscious mind is free to talk, plan and be rational. This means you can be riding at a show concentrating on your horse or talking to friends, and then become aware of a loose horse and bring your own horse under more control very quickly – your unconscious mind probably picked up the incident as it was starting to happen, which is how you are able to respond so effectively.

Unconscious experience?

Tell someone to put their left hand up in the air: they can do it in less than a second. Is this a conscious or unconscious action? Most people will answer conscious. However, to lift your left arm, you have to coordinate over 240 muscles, decide what is up and what is down, identify which is left and right and move a hand rather than a foot! Like our choice of words (see p.54), through years of experience, the unconscious mind has streamlined such actions so that we do not need to think consciously about what to do. It is very efficient at carrying out habitual tasks. Consider how easily you can tie up a haynet or put together a bridle now, compared to

the very first time you tried! However, this streamlining also means that less useful habits, like riding crookedly or feeling tense when you see a jump, and the attitudes behind them, can also become entrenched.

Think about the times you have driven home, along a familiar route, and suddenly realised you are nearly there but you can't remember going through certain towns and villages. Were you asleep? Did you miss all those police cars with their blue lights behind you? How many accidents did you have? The answers are no, no and none! You were simply leaving it to your unconscious to drive you from A to B. If there had been any incidents, they would have been drawn to your conscious attention. In an 'emergency' the unconscious will make the conscious aware of new signals. This explains how you can stay on when your horse spins and spooks at a pheasant or a paper bag even if moments before you were lolling along on a loose rein.

Being able to trust the unconscious or intuitive mind to respond appropriately is another skill to develop: good riders often don't know how they do certain things because they don't let their conscious mind get in the way!

Memory and the senses

For each of our memories, the mind has stored the detail experienced by each sense when the memory was made. By bringing out this detail, it is possible to re-experience a good memory and make it even better, and to change a disappointing memory. **In NLP, the senses are called modalities and their particular qualities are sub modalities.** Understanding these help you to understand your memories.

The qualities of the senses (sub modalities)

Each of our senses (modalities) has a series of perceptual qualities (sub modalities), a range between two opposites, such as colour to black-and-white, hard to soft, loud to quiet. The key sub modalities for seeing, feeling and hearing are shown here. They can help people identify how they have structured a memory and their use is a key part of building up resourceful states and anchors (see pp.86 and 87). In the examples, the word 'location' relates to place: where the picture is in your memory (up, down, right, left) or where the sound is coming from (behind, in front, left or right).

Sight and vision

People sometimes say that they cannot visualise – but actually everyone can. How do you recognise your horse or drive to the yard? Certainly not by using your senses of touch, hearing or smell! Often the thought that you cannot visualise is a hangover from school, a limiting belief about being creative.

When you think of a memory are you watching yourself in it (**disassociated**) or are you part of the scene (**associated**)? The words you use may be revealing: dissociated phrases include being 'out of it', 'on the sidelines', 'out of touch', while associated phrases include being 'in the thick of it', 'caught up in the action', 'all there'.

Think about other aspects of your picture. Is it still or moving? Is it in colour or black and white?

How big is your picture? Are you near or far away? In focus all the time? Where is it located?

Brightness:	Dim ...... Bright
Size:	Large ...... Small
Colour:	Black-and-White ...... Colour
Movement:	Fast ... Slow ... Still
Distance:	Near ...... Far
Focus:	Clear ...... Fuzzy
Your position:	Associated ...... Disassociated
Location	Where is the picture?

Sound and hearing

Listen to the sounds you remember and try to note the detail. If it is a voice, who's is it, and where does it come from? Are there thudding hooves, the creak of leather, sounds of the horse breathing, a commentary from someone, your own quiet commands to yourself?

Pitch:	High ...... Low
Volume:	Loud ...... Soft
Tempo:	Fast ...... Slow
Distance:	Near ...... Far
Tone:	Bass ...... Treble
Location	Where is the sound?

Feelings and movement

With a feeling, where does it start in your body, what temperature does it have, what texture is it? Recall how you were while taking part in an event: your posture in the saddle, the feeling of the reins, your weight in the stirrups.

Movement:	Moving ...... Still
Density:	Hard ...... Soft
Texture:	Smooth ...... Rough
Weight:	Heavy...... Light
Temperature:	Hot ...... Cold
Location:	Where is the feeling?

Exercise 19:
Prove it to yourself

The idea of subtle ways of storing memories is one of the biggest contributions that NLP has made to psychology. To reorganise memories for yourself, work through this exercise, perhaps with a friend. Pick a quiet time and place where you are likely to be left in peace.

1 Think about an event in which you were very successful or a lesson when you did very well or a lovely hack on a beautiful day – a special memory or magic moment. Think about what you recall, maybe talk about it until you start to really remember the event, including the details of what happened before or afterwards. In order for you to recall it fully, your mind will go back to how it was stored.

2 It may be helpful for your friend to ask you the following questions about your memory. What is the very first thing you remember? What did it look like? What did it feel like? What did you hear? Then use the questions in Exercise 20 to elicit more detail.

3 Run backwards and forwards through your memory a couple of times to notice the sequence. It could be that you hear yourself saying 'that was fantastic', as you see yourself jump the final fence. Or maybe you feel the warmth of the sun and the rush of the wind against your face as you gallop along the beach, hearing your horse's hoof beats in a rhythm. Write down some details about your memory for later exercises.

Exercise 20: What thoughts are behind your words?

Below are some different ways of saying things. Read them and choose which you like best. Which group of words do you use most often? They are all examples of the different ways that we represent memories and ideas to ourselves and they reveal whether we prefer one sensory system over another. Riders are often kinaesthetic, whereas musicians tend to be auditory and painters are visual. NLP calls the language of the senses VAK language (Visual, Auditory, Kinaesthetic).

Kinaesthetic (feeling) language	Visual language	Auditory language
'You're really getting to grips with this.'	'Do you get the picture…?'	'Listen to the horse's hoof beats.'
'Feel that trot.'	'Is that clearer?'	'Go in time with the rhythm.'
'Relax into the movement.'	'Imagine what that looks like.'	'Tell him to go forward.'
'Sit deeper.'	'Look at his ears.'	Words and voice used in a rhythmic way eg 'one, two, three; one, two, three.'
'Soften your hands.'	'Do you see what I mean?'	
	'Notice how much better that would look to a judge.'	

Having read about sub modalities, now think of alternative ways of saying the phrases in the table below. After all, you may be mainly kinaesthetic, but can you explain what you 'feel' to someone who prefers 'seeing' or 'hearing'? (This is particularly important for instructors.) The first row of boxes has been filled in as an example.

Kinaesthetic	Visual	Auditory
'Have you grasped the idea?'	'Is that clear?'	'Does that explain it to you?'
'Feel the rhythm.'		
		'Get in tune with each other.'
	'What would it look like if you were riding like the world champion?'	
	'Look at the line to the fence?'	

Exploring your sub modalities

When you want to identify sub modalities, these are the sorts of questions to ask.

What is felt when the experience is remembered?	What is seen in the memory?	What is heard in the memory?
Describe the feeling.	Where is it?	What can you hear?
Where does the feeling start?	Is it colour or black and white?	Where is the sound coming from?
What temperature is it?	Is is still or moving?	How loud is it?
What sort of texture is it?	If moving, how fast or slow compared to normal?	How clear is it?
How does it move?	Are you seeing it as if you were there or are you watching yourself in it?	What is the tone like?
Where does it move to?	How big is it?	How distinct is it?
How fast is it moving?	Is there a frame around it?	If it is a voice, whose is it?
What direction is it moving in?	Is it bright and sharp or dull and soft?	

Exercise 21: Spotting language patterns

Since your speech is an expression of the way you think, it follows that if you speak the same way as someone else, you will gain greater rapport. Learn more about how to spot someone's sensory processes by reading through the extracts opposite, which come from Mark Todd's autobiography *So Far, So Good*. You will get a good idea of how Mark sees the world, what motivates him, which senses he likes to work in, and some of his beliefs. For instance, he is more stimulated by his kinaesthetic sense than his visual ones, and relies little on his auditory senses. He also tends to be motivated away from problems, and is quite internally referenced. These two motivation traits influence his beliefs, and the generalisations, deletions and distortions he makes to maintain his confidence and performance.

In the passages, some of the language patterns, beliefs, sensory language, metaphors and meta-programmes are indicated as follows:

Metaphors are in *italic*; Beliefs are underlined; Generalisations, deletions and distortions are indicated in the right-hand column; VAK language is marked: (V) = Visual, (A) = Auditory, (K) = Kinaesthetic, (A ID) = Auditory/Internal dialogue.

This is an advanced exercise to demonstrate the mass of information contained in our everyday language. To develop this still further, attend NLP courses and review the books in the Bibliography (p.140).

Kwa'Chon racecourse had mountains in the background, just like Santa Anita, and the organisers had made it very attractive(V), with flags and flowers and bright colours(V). From the moment Podge (Charisma) arrived, *everything seemed to fit into place*(K), as if he knew this was his big moment. To do it justice he was feeling(K), and going(K), incredibly well… Staging a repeat Olympic bid obviously(A ID) brings *a measure of pressure*(K), but it was relieved a bit (K), because so many people thought(A ID) Podge was *past his peak*. In any case you never go into a competition thinking(A ID) 'I've got this one *sewn up*', no matter how well your horse is feeling(K).

Procedures
Mind read
Generalisation
Away from motivation
Deletion
Away from motivation

From the moment I got on Podge I was able to ride him(K) exactly as I wanted and he gave his best performance ever, going into the lead on 37.6…

Internally referenced
Procedures
Disassociated

Although Podge had a lower penalty score at Luhmuhlen in 1986, dressage marking is always subjective and I believe that the Seoul test was even better. The Horse and Hound dressage correspondent, the late Pegotty Henriques, clearly(V) agreed with me because she wrote, 'The test they showed(V) together was as good as you need to see(V) at this level and probably more faultless than the Grand Prix Special that the gold medallists Uphoff and Rembrandt performed.' She wasn't alone in her opinion because *a lot of people* said(A) that Podge should have been further in the lead…

Generalisation
Mind read

External support for internal referencing

After that I let him cruise(K) at his own pace and each time I checked(V), he was *up on the clock*, I took all the direct routes with the exception of Chosun's Choice, a combination fence, with a rail to a wide left-hand corner. Podge had run out(K) at a left-hand corner a year or so earlier at Gatcombe and I wasn't prepared to take the risk, especially when the longer way didn't waste much time. He jumped(K) everything immaculately and effectively *reduced the Olympic track to a Pony Club course*. When I asked(A) him to gallop over the final uphill fences, he was off(K) and he finished full of running(K) in the fastest time of the day. *Show off* that he was, he pulled up in extended trot(K), as if to say(A), 'Beat that if you can'… So much for being too old to compete!

Procedures

Away from motivation

Mind read

I knew he would rattle(K) the jumps if he wanted to, but I'd come to believe that the more relaxed(K) he was, the less likely they were to fall(K). Working on this principle I kept my warm-up(K) to a minimum so he wouldn't get excited(K). He started carefully(K) enough, but then he knocked(K) the first element of the treble and *the heat was on*(K). He rattled(K) the eighth hard and I had to *resist the temptation* to look back(V) and see(V) if it had stayed up. Fortunately it had and by the time I had got to the last two fences, I knew I could have them down and still win. *I felt like letting go*(K) and galloping at them out of sheer relief(K), but again *I resisted temptation*(K) and he jumped them clear. In the end he beat(K) Sir Wattie by 10.20 penalties, an unusually large margin for a major three day event.

Mind read

Procedures

Internal referencing

Procedures

Use the power of your mind

Make your good memories…
even better

The most effective thinking uses the 'critical' sub modalities – this means those sub modalities that are most important to you. You can find out which sub modalities are your critical ones by doing the exercises on the following pages.

As Helen's story (right) shows, perhaps the most powerful impact of NLP is the way it makes you aware of how easy it is to put yourself in control of your thoughts and the responses they generate. Usually we store good experiences with one set of sub modalities and bad ones differently.

Our best experiences are often large, colour, moving pictures, with pleasing sounds and feelings associated with them (this amount of emphasis should be reserved for your best memories so that you can regenerate great feelings whenever you want). When we get it the wrong way around, with our bad experiences as huge full-colour movies with special effects and all the drama, creating scary or stressful feelings, it's not surprising that we start thinking twice about doing that activity. It also explains why a bad experience can change our ability to do something, even though our rational part understands it is simply a past event. The way you store a memory affects your emotional and

exercise

Exercise 22: Finding your critical sub modalities

The most effective changes to thinking use the 'critical' sub modalities. Did you notice that some of the questions in exercise 19 (Prove it to yourself) had more impact than others, that some made the feeling even better? This is because these are affecting what are called your critical sub modalities.

1 Look at your answers to exercise 19. Get your friend to work through them again, this time asking what happens when they are varied. For instance, if your picture was small, what is it like to make it bigger? If it had a frame, what is it like without the frame?

2 After each question, your partner should make sure that the modality is returned to where it started (so if your picture was small and you made it big, it should be returned to small again before you continue), but note the ones that made the experience even better. You will find that certain changes have a bigger impact than others, these are the 'critical' sub modalities.

3 Take the most effective sub modalities, one from each modality – visual, auditory and kinaesthetic – and use all of them together to boost the memory. For example, supposing you found that making the picture bigger, adding more warmth to the feeling and softening the sounds individually improved the memory. Do all three at the same time and notice how it 'super improves' the memory. This teaches you how to drive your own experiences, which can then be used to really motivate you.

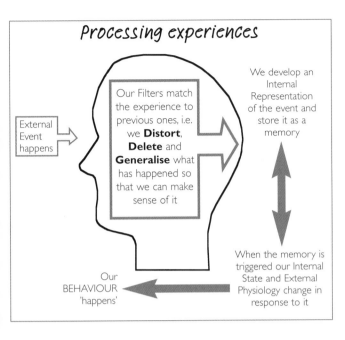

Processing experiences

External Event happens

Our Filters match the experience to previous ones, i.e. we **Distort**, **Delete** and **Generalise** what has happened so that we can make sense of it

We develop an Internal Representation of the event and store it as a memory

When the memory is triggered our Internal State and External Physiology change in response to it

Our BEHAVIOUR 'happens'

physiological state: your heart beat will change and your skin will flush and this will affect how you behave (see diagram).

So, how does it work? Since both memory and imagination share the same circuitry – the same brain and the nerve endings through your body – one can affect the other. This is why visualisation (see p.80), self-talk (p.60) and the importance of correct practice to put a learning 'into a muscle' is so important in improving your ability. (Where you have really become set in a pattern, get an experienced NLP coach to help you swap around the sub modalities and identify what resources you need to progress again.)

Case study: Helen's critical sub modalities

case study

This case study illustrates how making simple changes can be powerful in enhancing a memory. On a recent course Helen volunteered to discuss her special memory.

She was jumping at a local show. Her memory picture was in colour and was of horse and rider from the side, caught in mid-air over the jump. It was a fairly small picture and about 5 metres away. There was no sound or no particular feelings. When I asked Helen whether or not she was smiling in her picture, she had to lean forwards and peer – and remember this was when it was just in her mind!

I suggested she imagined the picture closer, about three feet away. There was a transformation. Helen could 'see' that she was smiling. I then suggested that she made the picture into a film. The picture began moving in slow motion. So I suggested she made it larger, up to lifesize. Her face lit up as she took it all in. **Now she could hear the horse, his hooves and breathing, and her friends cheering.**

She was literally bouncing in her chair as she remembered it! With the sub modality changes and as the picture became larger, Helen had automatically

swapped from a dissociated memory into an associated memory, where she was imagining it as if it was really happening, so that she could see the horse's ears in front of her and the course and feel each stride and jump. **By bringing it to life again she was able to realise how much she had enjoyed jumping,** and she booked a lesson for later that week. Although she was only 40 years old, she had never expected to jump again – and she was thrilled to have 'got back the old feeling'.

see also:
Associated and disassociated p.69

'Suddenly I could vividly see myself jumping with a big smile and hear myself say 'Yes' at each fence. Soon afterwards I went to a local show and jumped two rounds, even getting a rosette, and really enjoyed it again. And all I had to do was think of jumping and smiling.'

Exercise 23: Change a negative memory

This exercise works by adjusting your sub modalities and can help you alter an unsatisfactory memory and use it positively.

1 Take a mildly unpleasant situation that has happened to you in the past. For example, working through a schooling problem. (Save the bigger issues for later exercises!)

2 As you think through your example, notice what sort of sounds come to mind, or if it is completely quiet.

3 As you are doing this you will stimulate your visual memory. If you get a still picture start to run it like a film. Begin by viewing it fairly slowly, just one still picture after another, and build on this until you can move from one picture to the next in slow motion, then in normal speed and finally in fast forward mode.

4 Once you have the film running at whatever speed is right for you, notice how you feel as you watch it. At this stage you will probably feel fairly flat or fed up — after all it is a problem state.

5 Now choose some music for your film. Pick something like a motivating pop song. Hear this music loud and powerfully in your mind, then watch your film again, with the music playing all the way through.

6 As a test, play the film without the music — notice how you feel now. Usually the memory reduces in intensity — it doesn't matter so much — or is neutralised or has even become humorous.

Having changed the feeling, notice that you can now watch your film and think about what you would do differently. Experiment with different pieces of music until you find one that works best for you. As you get used to doing it, you will find that you can play the music in your head as your ride and that this will help you as you handle different situations.

Case study: A change of voice

Lyn found that as she reached more advanced levels of competition having worked in well, she would ride up the centre line, halt, salute — and then this doom-laden voice would say 'You shouldn't be here'.

In a short session, we identified that the voice was an earlier instructor, who didn't want Lyn to show herself up by competing above her level. **The voice was still playing, even though Lyn was now well up to the appropriate standard.**

I asked Lyn to imagine herself in the competition situation and this time make the voice comical as it said the phrase. Mickey Mouse was her choice — and she suddenly laughed as she experienced the difference. **As she imagined riding up the centre line, the laughing had made her more relaxed immediately.** Next, she imagined cantering up the centre line and this time she heard the same words said in a sexy man's voice. That had the effect of making her laugh too — and want to show that 'Oh yes, I should be here'.

Using this simple technique Lyn has let go of the old voice and can carry on and ride to the best of her ability.

Case study: A change of picture

Mel loved working with horses and planned to take her British Horse Society exams with a view to becoming a level one International Instructor. However, when she came to jump, or even think about it, even the smallest fence looked like a huge brick wall. And it was definitely not jumpable!

She came along to an introductory course for instructors and volunteered to work with me to demonstrate how NLP helps to change such unwanted behaviour. **We started with Mel describing the imaginary jump, going into some detail about how high it was and the colour of the bricks – this developed her visual imagination.** We made it higher and wider and then put it back to its original size – this gently loosened up the 'stuck' thinking: the imagination is a wonderfully quick at making such changes.

I then asked Mel to look more closely and realise that, in fact, the bricks were so perfect in their repeating pattern that they had to be wallpaper. The earlier work of stretching the jump to being bigger and wider had brought the image to Mel's conscious attention and, therefore, into her control. So, what would she do with the wall now? We considered whether she should set fire to it or jump through it, like they do at the police

horse demonstrations. She decided that she would dowse it with water until it became a soggy mass.

With 'the jump' dissolved, Mel was now able to think about jumping in a really positive manner and happily booked a lesson for the next day. Everyone in the room could see that she meant it, she was so happy: her old fear really had gone in the space of 10 minutes. She rang me the next day to say how well the lesson had gone, how the old brick wall had never even appeared and how much she had enjoyed being able to jump again.

A few weeks later Mel passed her preliminary exam and several months later rang to say that she had just completed the next stage successfully – she was well on track for her goal.

Case study:
A change of feeling

Jane was a leading young dressage rider who was starting to feel blocked when she competed. Closer questioning about the sub modalities of the 'thing' blocking her revealed it was like a heavy ball of gloom, a football-sized dark blue-black ball.

Notice the detail of this metaphor – it is the starting point to work with: Jane could hardly ride well with that in her stomach, especially as dressage is all about getting softness!

I asked Kate about the ball's texture. Given that it was heavy, it was not surprising that she said it was hard and textured. **I asked her to check the ball's positive intent and it was about being very serious and important** – it was how she stored 'serious'. With that insight we could work to lighten and soften the ball so that it could help her be taken even more seriously. This is because it was important to get softness and lightness in her riding. By making softness and lightness as important as hardness, she could be more serious about her riding. The play on words

creates the right reframe of this situation.

Jane was able to work on changing the ball's texture and to lighten it by squeezing out all the dead weight. She imagined it one way then the other – lighter to heavier and back again, several times. Then we considered what colour it was now – it was a lighter, softer blue, more like a cloud. **The final part was to decide where to put this cloud-like ball. Jane chose to imagine it in the small of her back.** There it could drive her forward and up to be light and soft.

Jane won her first Intermediare 1 a couple of weeks later. She said she had found the session 'amazingly helpful' and that everything she had been working towards just all came together on the day.

see also:
Positive intent p.60
Reframing pp.63–64

Seeing yourself as a better rider 9

It is only through imagination that men become aware of what the world might be. Bertrand Russell

Visualisation

'Imagination is more important…
than knowledge.'*

Visualisation can be used to create dreams, imagine their outcomes and see their longer term effects. One of the core tools in NLP, it is used in several of the change techniques (see pp.127–139). In the outcome process (p.14), when you **imagine a dream in your mind's eye** and the result is satisfactory to you, you can then **recognise and mobilise the resources** (p.86) needed to **turn that dream into a reality**.

Visualisation is the way we form mental images: memories, fantasies or a combination of both. It can include all of the senses – seeing, hearing, feeling, smell and taste. As visualisation occurs in the nervous system, it can directly influence our body. Certain types of visualisation can even stimulate the functioning of our immune system and other healing processes. In setting outcomes or goals the visualisation acts as an 'attractor' around which our behaviour becomes organised.

Exercise 24: Simple steps to the perfect visualisation

1 Imagine what it will be like to achieve your goal.

2 Check that is OK for you to achieve it – that you have no little worries about winning. If necessary address any worries with the outcome process (p.14).

3 Imagine it as if you are watching someone else achieving it (this is called third position, see p.96) – maybe a famous rider or your instructor.

4 When you have seen, heard and felt what it is like for someone who is a better rider to do it well, imagine it as if you are that rider. Add as much detail as you can and be associated with the experience – see your horse's neck and ears in front of you, feel the reins in your hands, hear his hoof beats. Enjoy the feeling – this is what it is like when you are doing your best.

5 Run through step 4 at least five times, until it becomes natural. You can keep improving it if you like! Anchor the feeling too – see p.87.

*Albert Einstein

Tips for powerful visualisations

● Aim to make your visualisation as life-like as possible. In this way you can mentally experience all the necessary physical micro-muscular movements. It follows that you will visualise these movements most successfully if you have experienced them before.

● Identify your critical sub modalities (see p.74). Adjust your visualisation to incorporate these.

● Be associated (see p.69) into the event you are visualising, otherwise it will not be life-like enough. Use your peripheral vision within your life-size picture: as you look ahead in your imagination, through the horse's ears, what are you aware of to your left and right?

● Hear the sounds that would be there, include any constructive self-talk (p.60–61).

● For important visualisations, imagine being the judges, selectors, examiners or even other competitors so that you can understand what it is like for them (second positioning, see p.96). This will give you valuable insights into other resources you could add into your visualisation – perhaps it would help if you behaved in a different way towards your fellow competitors, for instance?

● Where you aren't comfortable with elements of your visualisation, or where you imagine a huge range of things that might happen, run through each scenario, seeing yourself respond effectively and coping with the situation. Then run through the perfect visualisation again and again.

Case study:
A winning combination

Christilot Boylen rode in her first Olympic Games at the age of just 17 and went on to ride for Canada in another six Olympics. She was introduced to the value of sports psychology at the Montreal Olympics in 1976, where, not surprisingly, as the best of the Canadians, she had a big build up with a lot of pressure.

To make matters more than worse, her horse pulled a check ligament in the weeks beforehand, limiting his training. **Because the team coach wanted to keep the situation secret, she had to worry alone.** Her nerves became very frayed – after all the whole country's hopes were riding on her back.

Luckily for Christilot, she was sent on a course of visualisation, and there she realised that even if everything did all go wrong on the day, she would not actually commit suicide but just get on with riding the horses. She realised that the consequences were not nearly so bad as she was imagining them.

She went on to learn the visualisation techniques, which were particularly useful as her horse had not been competed outdoors for some time due to the injury. She visualised a flowing test, her concentration so high that it felt like it was in slow motion. **With this extraordinary preparation – no trot, no canter, no real dressage – it was incredible that she finished sixth in the Olympic Grand Prix.**

Afterwards Christilot commented 'The test did flow, that performance was high above any other I had done. Nobody knew the difficulties behind the ride.'

'The sports psychology training was crucial. I had already been doing some of the things they taught me, but it was the degree that you could take it to and the consistency you could reach that was important.'

Case study: Sorting out exam nerves

Jo had previously failed her Preliminary Riding exam, despite having been told she was well above standard. She was, therefore, very anxious about retaking the exam, to the extent that, as the day got closer, she felt very sick.

She spent her time worrying about what might happen, which is a sure way of attracting a bad experience. She imagined making a mistake and freezing up so that the whole day would descend into a disaster. As one of her instructors, I knew how important the exam was to her.

The evening before the exam, we had a session in which she visualised the next day. Having already been up to the exam centre for a lesson, she could imagine the layout, and having been through the exam she knew the format of the day. We started by setting up an anchor for staying calm and confident, so she could have this feeling at any point in the day that she needed it.

Rather than just imagining a perfect exam, I then asked Jo to imagine the sorts of things that would she would do, building in the important exam techniques such as checking stirrup leathers, noting what tack the horse was wearing, looking around at other candidates when riding in open order, listening attentively to the instructions and relating to the horse in a sensitive way. All of these details were important. Then we added in the little errors that could happen, like striking off on the wrong leg or refusing a fence. We visualised how she would cope with them: what she would do to correct the mistake, then how she would stay calm and unflustered and what she would say to the examiner afterwards.

Next, we imagined what it was like to be the examiners, seeing it from their perspective. **Jo found this very surprising: the examiners actually wanted to pass the candidates. They were not ogres at all.**

We ran through the visualisation as if we were watching a film a few times, with Jo noticing where she needed to improve and then discussing what she would do differently. Then she 'stepped in the film', imagining it actually happening to her step-by-step.

As I saw her happy relaxed expression and confident stance I knew she would pass. She did more than that, she got a pass plus, and she was thrilled.

As Jo explains: 'Rationally, I found it easy to visualise passing, but found it difficult to actually believe it deep down. It was only when we ran through the visualisation of the whole exam, slowed down with all the detail, that I could believe it. Then I felt calm and confident that I could sort out anything that went wrong on the day.'

She reflected: 'I realised I had been fooling myself everything was alright, yet I needed to face my deep-rooted problem of exam nerves and deal with them. And it was a fun way of sorting it out. Liz made me laugh as we worked it out and I really enjoyed the exam.'

see also:
Anchoring p.86
Second positioning p.96

Jo's story illustrates that the NLP approach to visualisation is much more than positive thinking, or saying unrealistic affirmations to yourself. It can bring you back to your best performance, time after time, leaving you ready to learn how to get even better.

Exercise 25:
A starring role

This exercise is an introduction to using visualisation techniques for future events. It is based on things you have already achieved.

1 Take three or four events from your list of achievements (exercise 7, p.27) and describe each event like a story in a few words. Add in why this was important to you, what you learned for the future and other important aspects. Now imagine that you are going to direct a documentary of you achieving all those things. Think about the beginning sequences, the middle, then the end. You may choose to have a partner who can make suggestions to prompt you as you go.

2 Be disassociated (see p.69), seeing yourself in the role in a detached way, then edit and weave each achievement together to make the documentary. Start with the background to the story behind one achievement, then go on to the background to the next, and the next, and so on. In particular, notice the resources you are demonstrating in each storyline. It may be confidence, calmness, tolerance. Hear the narrator's voice explaining to the audience about these characteristics, and about any challenges you had to face to get to this point.

3 Move into the middle part of each event: what happened, how it felt to be that person facing that situation, then to be the same person facing the other two or three situations. Add comments on what other people involved thought about the situation – you know what makes a good documentary!

4 Then move on to after the event when the success has been achieved. Think about what each achievement meant to you and others. What were the common themes between them?.

5 Run through your documentary several times, choose some theme music and a title that really captures the spirit of the person in the documentary. Now, step into the role, be fully associated (see p.69), and run through it again; enjoy being that person. Run through a few times until you can really appreciate yourself. Play the theme tune any time you want to feel really good.

See how powerfully good memories can work to boost your confidence and esteem? Now imagine what it would be like to use this exercise as a starting point for a visualisation about something you want to achieve in the future.

Making the most of your resources

Once you understand how a horse communicates,
you can understand how he thinks.
Once you understand how he thinks,
you can understand what's important to him.
And that's the key. Mark Rashid

Being resourceful

Be confident, calm and determined...
whenever you want to be

Anchoring is a technique that **allows you to call up a useful psychological state or resource** such as **confidence, calmness or determination**, whenever you need it. We all already have many anchors. For instance, when you hear your name said in a certain tone, or see a photo of a special event, it will bring up **details of the memory and the feeling** that you had then. Useful (resourceful) feelings can be brought back when you need them simply by **giving yourself a signal** such as digging your fingers into your palm or thinking of a word or phrase. People are amazed at how **quickly and effectively this works**.

The technique is also the first step to take when tackling an emotion that has become inappropriately attached to a particular situation. For example, where someone has lost confidence when jumping or where they get nervous before a dressage test, they can break the negative cycle by changing states, which is done by firing a 'resourceful' anchor (see p.87). Once they have changed their emotional state, say from nervousness to calmness, the horse can follow. (See also *What are resourceful states?*, opposite.)

exercise

Exercise 26:
Find your resources

This exercise helps you to identify your resources, from all aspects of your life, and to become aware of the resources you need to achieve your goal. Anchoring (opposite) explains how you can use your resourceful experiences to really improve your riding. Write down the resources you have available to you – many will help you towards your goal. Write down a wish list of the resources you need, too. They could include the following:

- *Supported by friends*
- *Feel good about myself*
- *Experience of riding to a certain standard*
- *Sound basic training*
- *Relaxed with horses*
- *Desire to learn more*
- *Open mindedness*
- *Calmness in a crisis*
- *Determination*
- *Tenacity*

Now look at your list of achievements (exercise 7, p.27). Review the list and think about the resources each experience gave you. Some may have given you similar resources, while others may have brought you a whole string of different ones. It is also helpful to identify the various resources you use in different aspects of your daily life, at work, with the family. Compare the lists of resources you already have and those you need – the chances are that somewhere in your life, you have experienced the resource you now need for your riding.

Exercise 27:
Setting up an anchor

Setting up an anchor is straightforward, although it is often helpful to have a friend take you through the steps so that you can just concentrate on the memories.

1	**Choose a resource you want more of.**	This could be confidence, calmness, determination, assertiveness…something inside you that would make you feel good in a situation.
2	**Remember a time when you had a real experience of that feeling. Talk about it.**	It could be as a child, at work, on holiday or while riding. Check that the experience had a happy ending. Step forward and remember the experience, telling your friend about it in some detail, as if it was happening to you now (associated, p.69). They can ask you questions to make it more alive, such as who else was there, what you saw, and heard, and how you felt. Your friend should avoid commenting on your experience or sharing their own – they can just nod and agree and be interested!
3	**'Break state' – return to the here and now.**	Your friend should direct you to break out of your memory by asking you a question about something completely different, like the colour of the carpet! This is called the 'break state' and is an important element of the process.
4	**Decide what three signals you will give yourself to recall the resource.**	Make one a physical signal (thumb pressing on forefinger or fingers digging into palm), one visual (an image you associate with the resource), and one a word or phrase or line from a song you can say to yourself. They should be simple and easy to 'fire' while you are in the situation you want the resourceful state in. Make them something you can do when riding.
5	**Go back into the memory.**	Your friend can prompt you with the words you used to describe it. When the memory feels really good and strong, give yourself the signal, say the word or phrase to yourself and see the image, all together. Hold them and then break out of the memory.
6	**Repeat step 5 two or three more times.**	Remember to 'break state' between each. What you are doing is like finding your way to a new address. Each time you do it, it becomes quicker and easier, until you can get there with just a simple signal.
7	**Imagine a time in the future when you would like this feeling.**	Tell your friend about it as you imagine it, then just fire the anchor and notice what feels different.

The more you use your anchor – being sure to use the same words, signal and image – the stronger it will become. After a while one element such as just the touch or the word will be sufficient to take you to that great feeling, every time.

What are resourceful states?

In NLP a resource is anything that helps you reach a desired state or resolve a problem state. Resources may be environmental opportunities, behaviours, skills or capabilities, internal emotional states, empowering beliefs, even a strong sense of identity or spirituality. You can take an ability (resource), you have in another area of your life, such as confidence at work or patience with children, and add it to your riding, too.

Quick tips for effective anchors

- Certain parts of the body, such as the hand or earlobes, have more nerve endings and so are better places to set up your anchor. Useful anchors are pressing the thumb nail into a specific finger, pinching your earlobe or digging your nails into your palm.

- Involve the three main senses together: a word or phrase (auditory), a picture or symbol (visual) and a kinaesthetic signal, such as pinching your thumb and finger together.

Stacked anchors

Sometimes it's useful to have several resources all together at the same time, such as confidence, calmness, sensitivity and determination. Set up four anchors on the same hand by the thumb pressing onto each finger – one finger for each resource state. Once these have been set up and tested, fire them in quick succession by running the thumb across the four fingers. It's great!

case study

Case study: Lizzie appreciates her abilities

Lizzie was a rider who tended to be very negative about herself and her riding ability, and too often her rides seemed to go wrong. She was losing confidence and the desire to continue with her riding.

She was also a senior nurse in an accident and emergency ward where she had implemented some major initiatives to improve patient care. She had a lot of job satisfaction and loved her work. When we talked about this, she realised that she felt valued and confident, because she knew she was doing the right thing. **She was also very 'in the moment', able to respond to whatever came up, knowing that she knew the work well and could carry the responsibility.** There were a number of episodes that related to each resourceful state. These were all things that she would love to have when she rode, too. We decided to link these feelings into a series of anchors for her riding.

She recalled something at work that had given her a number of resources, of which we chose four: feeling valuable, having confidence, being able to respond calmly to any situation, and trusting her knowledge. We

see also:
*Setting up an anchor
p.87
Stacked Anchors (above)*

anchored the first by pressing the thumb onto the first finger of the left hand, the second onto the second finger, the third onto the ring finger and then the fourth onto the little finger. Each one was set up using the anchoring process, so it took a few minutes to re-live each feeling. **At the end Lizzie was able to fire off each anchor in rapid succession by running her thumb across her four fingers, a simple gesture that felt amazing and is now a powerful resource in itself whenever she wants to have those feelings!**

How would it help your riding if you could feel good about your ability, confident, able to respond calmly to any situation, and trust your own knowledge when you rode?

Exercise 28: Circle of excellence

By now you will have realised that a lot of your riding issues and previous barriers to improvement revolve around your level of confidence and self esteem. Use this exercise to draw on positive feelings from your past and bring them to where you need them now. The exercise is a development of anchoring using the physical experience of stepping into a defined space, which is known as spatial anchoring.

1 Stand up and remember a time when you felt very confident. Go through the memory, seeing what you saw, hearing what you heard and feeling what you felt. Identify the critical sub modalities (p.74). Now optimise them:

- *Take the feeling and make it even bigger or faster or stronger.*

- *See your picture and make it even better – maybe bigger or brighter or more colourful. Is it better as a still picture that captures the magic moment, or as a film? See yourself smiling and notice how your posture reflects your confidence.*

- *Now notice what you hear. Is it other peoples voices congratulating you, maybe it's the horse's hooves and breathing, or a voice inside your head saying 'Yes' or 'We've done it' or 'Good boy' or whatever. Notice the volume and tone of these sounds.*

2 Now that you have built up this feeling of confidence, imagine a circle around you on the floor. Choose a colour for it, see it shine and glimmer. Once the feeling is really alive, step out of the circle and shake it off – a physical break state (p.87).

3 Think about a time in the future when you want that feeling – just before you go in the ring or into an exam or going to try a new horse. Imagine what you will see and hear just before – in these examples it may be the entrance to the arena, the examiners coming in or the horse's head over the door.

4 Once you have these cues clear, step into the circle and feel those fantastic feelings. Imagine what you want to happen as you experience all the power of that confident feeling again. Spend time and use your imagination to add in all the details – what you will see hear and feel.

5 Step out of the circle and break state. Then think again about the forthcoming event. You'll find that the feelings are there with it. And when the event happens, you can respond just as confidently.

Exercise 29:
Collapsing anchors

This technique is valuable for changing behavioural habits, but will not be so effective for deeper issues or strongly held beliefs. It involves using two anchors, one for a resourceful state and the other for a problem situation, and then creating a psychological link between the two. This has the effect of merging the two patterns of behaviour into the same time and space in the mind, so creating a third pattern of behaviour. Jenny's case study (opposite) demonstrates how effective it is. The exercise is best undertaken with a friend.

1 Your friend starts by asking you about the resourceful situation where you had good feelings that are relevant to your current problem. Build this up to be powerful resource, a strong state, by finding the critical sub modalities (see p.74). When your friend has evoked enough good feelings, he or she anchors it on, say, your left hand or knee.

2 'Break state' (see Setting up an anchor, p.87) and repeat until the anchor is strong.

3 Now your friend asks about the unpleasant situation – just enough to be able to recreate it, not enough for it to become distressing. Again she or he anchors it using a different part of the body, such as the opposite hand or knee.

4 Break state and repeat another couple of times.

5 Your partner then alternately fires each anchor, to check that they work.

6 While holding the resourceful anchor, your partner fires and releases the negative anchor.

7 Get your friend to test the process by asking you about a situation in the future where previously you would have been unable to access the resourceful state. She or he should also fire the old negative anchor and ask what you feel there – you should just experience the new resourceful feeling.

Case study:
Jumping for joy – again!

Jenny used to love jumping, but a series of incidents had left both her and her mare nervous at the thought of it. The horse would sweat and start napping, if they went near the jumps in their schooling field. Of course, this also made Jenny tense and nervous and the problem just escalated.

It was important to break the cycle with a change of states. In our first session together I asked Jenny to remember a time when she had really enjoyed jumping – a magic moment.

She described it to me and by asking questions about it, we intensified the memory. Then we 'anchored' it so that whenever she pressed her thumb onto her forefinger, the memory and the feeling would come back. I could tell it had by the way her posture changed and her face lit up. **By firing this anchor during the lesson Jenny was able to keep the good memory as she came to the jumping area.** The horse, of course, picked up Jenny's new-found confidence and relaxation, so she also calmed down and relaxed significantly and we were able to work over both trot and canter poles. As we moved to

small jumps, Jenny admitted that she was seeing a horrible image of crashing among poles, which was interfering with the good anchor we had set up. I therefore anchored the bad memory through talking about it. **Then, by firing the good and bad anchors in a certain sequence, we collapsed the bad one so that all she had left was the good one of flying over the fence.** This technique makes the mind jumble up and lose the old picture. It took 5–10 minutes and left Jenny incredulous!

'I can't believe it. It's just gone', she said. Try as she might, she couldn't get the horrible image back either!

They finished that session with some low jumps approached in trot and canter, huge smiles on both their faces.

Know your horse

'Ask the very beasts…
and they will answer.'*

A knowledge of the horse's sensory experience is valuable when riding and relating to them. Along with other animals, **horses have the same five senses as us** – seeing, hearing, touch, smell and taste. While there are similarities in the way they use these, there are also differences that have evolved mainly due to their way of life.

First and foremost the horse's view of the world is shaped by 'danger'. It has many millions of years of experience of this written into its genes, and its whole raison d'etre is one of survival.

The far ancestors of horses lived in forested land. They evolved to leave the shelter of the trees for the grassy plains, but this move meant more danger from packs of predators. Therefore, their senses developed to enable them to be highly aware of predators, as did their physical ability to escape by galloping away

over uneven ground or to defend themselves by kicking or striking out with their legs.

Sight

The horse's eyes are very different from ours. They are the largest eyes of any land mammal, and, being set on the side of the head, they command nearly 360 degree vision. Their position high on the head means that the horse can graze in quite tall vegetation while still keeping watch for danger. However, as the horse's eyes are set on the side of his head he cannot perceive relative distances in the same way as predators (humans, cat family) with their front-facing eyes. Predators need three-dimensional sight (two eyes with their angles of vision diverging by only a few degrees) to judge exactly where their prey is at the moment of attack.

When a horse puts his head up, he can see distant images in sharp focus, but closer images are not so clear. This explains why a horse will suddenly stop to look at an object at the periphery of his sight or lift his head high when he perceives movement on the horizon – he is changing the angle of vision to take a better look. So your horse has this incredible ability to see clearly at great distances, but a paper bag blown into the air close to his feet represents a poorly focused, unknown and, therefore, potentially dangerous, threat.

The horse sees in colour, although this is likely to

be in a form equivalent to colour-blindness in humans. In his appreciation of the world, he therefore relies more heavily on movement than colour. For instance, he will happily pass a camouflaged sitting rabbit or bird without fuss. But if there is the slightest movement, he reacts (after all, on the plains he could have been in real danger from a stalking predator or a striking snake).

Armed with this knowledge, we should not be annoyed at our horse reacting to a spooky object, but instead be calm and reassuring yet firm, so that the spook doesn't turn into running off. Once a horse runs for his life, everything he's learnt is temporarily forgotten. We need to reassure him that he is safe with us.

The horse's eye is highly light-sensitive and takes a

little time to adjust from shade to bright sunshine. When you go round a cross-country course, for example, he will probably experience several transitions from shade to brightness, so make allowance for this when you are walking the course. Horses can see better than humans at night, although the image is likely to be less focused than in daylight.

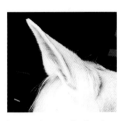

Hearing and vocal communication

In terms of communication, compared to other animals, and certainly humans, the horse has a limited vocal repertoire. It is mainly used for calling the herd's attention to danger, communication between mates, to assert dominance

Case study: Going back to nature

Andre Bourlet Slavkov, an anthropologist and classical riding instructor, has made a study of the horse's movement patterns and has applied his findings to help riders improve their riding.

Andre's research shows that two million years ago, which is short in terms of evolutionary development, human beings began to move on two legs. Our hands were free to become a fantastic tool. Gradually our brains developed programmes to use the tool and this became a cycle – standing on two legs became a way to develop the use of our hands and, therefore, develop the brain. However, by standing on two legs, we lost our understanding of four-legged locomotion, which is richer and more subtle than two-legged movement. Andre believes that four-legged movement also activates different pumps and rhythms in the body.

His theory is that the secret of good horse riding is the reawakening of the four-legged movement patterns that we contain genetically. After all we all start by crawling as children. Children also enjoy freedom of movement such as skipping and

dancing, but as we reach adulthood we tend to move much more towards the simple two-legged experience, which is more narrow than that of animals. Perhaps this is why riding is so attractive to so many of us.

Andre believes that if we mimic the way a horse moves – using our hands to represent the horse's forlegs – we can reactivate our understanding of four-legged movement. His unmounted workshops include practising the paces of the horse and becoming more aware of our own patterns of movement. When these are aligned with those of the horse, softer riding is possible.

Andre explains that at its most skilled, riding can be like giving a massage to the horse, and that the contact of the hands is paramount – where it is poor, it can be torture for the horse.

and by a mare and foal calling to each other. The sound travels a long way – a horse can whinny to another one so distant that we cannot see or hear it and certainly not smell it.

For closer herd communication situations, horses have developed a sophisticated visual-auditory system using fine control of the facial and ear muscles and gestures, and, of course, a whole body language. A horse's ears can be turned to give all-round hearing, which is important for a prey animal, and their movement also plays a significant role in body language. What a contrast to our own ears, which are always flat back against the sides of our heads, in what the horse may see as an aggressive gesture. Since we couple this with the both-eyes-forward stare of the typical meat-eating predator, it's no wonder we have to work to win his trust and confidence. Among the many ways to do this are by presenting yourself sideways-on when possible (to avoid direct eye contact) and to make sure your horse hears calm, reassuring talk from you.

Smell

Compared to horses, we are ignorant about smell and do not use this sense much at the conscious level. Smell and responses to odours play a complex part in the horse's mating and territorial behaviour, and smell is the sense by which the horse can find his way over long distances. Ensure that your odour is reassuringly consistent for your horse: the stables are not the place to try out that new perfume!

Taste

The horse is able to graze very selectively, probably combining smell with taste in order to choose what is grasped with his lips. He is well able to discriminate between tainted, spore-laden food and that which is good and fresh, and his feeding preferences should be respected. He is also able to detect contamination of food and therefore is certainly the best judge of your stable management!

Touch and kinaesthetics

The horse's skin and his ability to use it as a sensory system is more refined than ours – just watch a horse twitching a fly off his body. His whiskers are also very sensitive and enable him to feel for food – luckily the habit of shaving them off for the sake of appearance is fast dying out.

The horse's ability to travel at speed over uneven ground and around obstacles is hard-wired into his neurology. When you add to this his ability to balance himself, especially with a rider on board, it is obvious that he has a special form of 'intelligence'. However, a discussion of the horse's neurological and muscular systems, its proprioception so exquisitely tuned to every slightest change in muscle contraction, is outside the scope of this book.

Emotions and intuitions

I have been fortunate to work with Margrit Coates, a clairvoyant healer. She believes that horses have emotions, although they may be on a different level to humans and more relevant to their species. In *Healing For Horses* she writes of a lecture she gave to a riding club. She asked the audience for a list of human emotions and they came up with love, fear, hatred, anger, grief, resentment, jealousy, worry. She then asked which of these applied only to humans, and the room fell silent. If you know and love your horse, you know he has changing feelings. How much do you take them into account in your management of him?

Margrit says 'Emotions are not exclusive to humans and it is arrogant to think so. Horses have emotions and when they are denied the free expression of them or express negative emotions due to poor management, problems frequently occur, which we then often blame the horse for.'

And we can all think of times when our horse seems to mind read. The day before a show he becomes excited or he strikes off into canter before we have asked with the aids – these are indications of the horse's ability to respond to minute, sub-conscious clues that we give out. Certainly the horse is a very special animal.

Step into your horse's shoes

Horses are a great metaphor for our own personal development. They hold a mirror to us every day, reflecting every mental and emotional bobble! Horses have no concern for our egos. They tell it like it is, offering us the opportunity to develop the patience of Job, the courage of a lion tamer, the gentleness of a mother with her new born baby, the timing of a kung fu black belt and the focus of a world leader...

`The horse like no other living creature teaches us to become more than we are because until we are what he needs us to be, he'll give us mediocre results. *Pat Parelli*

Take a different perspective

Learn to see the world…
through the eyes of your horse

The benefit of understanding the difference between our senses and those of the horse (see p.92) is that we can **develop a level of communication** beyond that which we currently use. By being able to **'step into' the mind and body of your horse**, you will be able to **understand its reactions and respond** more calmly and appropriately.

Perceptual positions

In NLP putting yourself in someone else's shoes, or indeed your horse's shoes, is called using perceptual positions. There are three main positions and the core skill is called second positioning.

First position

First position is seeing things strictly from your own point of view, your feelings and emotions, your reasoning behind your choice of action, in short, what makes you tick. (The horse sees everything from the stance of first position!) It is the place from which to set goals and visualise your desired outcomes. Most people are perfectly good at first position skills – but unless they develop other positions, they can lack empathy with others. They may come across as rather self-centered and difficult to work with (yes, the horse is always in first position!).

Second position

In second position, you put yourself into the body and mindset of the person (or horse) by first studying their behaviour and body language. It is just like stepping into their shoes – the perfect place to gain a better understanding of their perspective – or having empathy with them. You become that other person or the horse – feeling what they feel, seeing what they see and hearing what they hear. Second positioning is the classic skill of good parents who are able to identify the needs of the young child based on their intuition and empathy. However, when someone uses second position too much, especially if it is to the exclusion of first position, they can lose their self esteem, because they give priority to others.

Third position

There is also a third, or observer, position. Here, you stand back, and take a completely rational view of the situation, detached from all the emotions involved. You imagine you are a fly on the wall or, better still, a wise old thing. It is a very useful `clinical' position to take when there is anger or frustration to contend with, since the whole situation can be reviewed dispassionately. It is also a valuable place to go to consider the knowledge you need to gain over a period of time. Used excessively, third position gives the impression of being detached and unemotional, unable to relate to the needs of others.

If you use all three positions in a balanced way you can gain useful insights into many situations, and identify and maintain what will be good for you as well as for others.

Using perceptual positioning

Imagine the following situation: you are learning with an instructor and going through a particularly difficult phase. It might be sensible to use second position to get a feeling of the problem from your instructor's point of view. Perhaps you are trying to achieve rather more than you or the horse are currently capable of? Perhaps your instructor thinks you are at fault by failing to be honest about your difficulties? By imagining being the instructor, you might find that he or she is really dispirited about this, and is finding it difficult to correct the problems without going back to square one.

Now, you could put yourself in third or observer position, and diagnose whether the faults are in you (for expecting too much) or in the instructor (who can't adjust his or her teaching methods to match your expectations) or, most probably, in both. From the perspective of third position, you can come up with suggestions for a better relationship.

Second positioning with people

You will be able to find many other situations in which perceptual positioning could be of help. Look at your horse, your work colleagues, your friends, and consider any conflicts you've had. Apply these principles to help you understand the causes and find possible remedies.

Second positioning is especially helpful when you are considering taking an exam, riding in front of judges, even choosing a horse, livery yard or instructor. However, remember that it is very different from mind reading – see distortion p.56.

As you develop second positioning skills, you will realise that our minds are as much on display as our physical bodies. When we are in second position with a person, we often realise that behaviour which seems totally out of order or very odd and unfriendly becomes meaningful and normal. In fact, the person is behaving in that way because, at the time, it is their best choice. Understanding this in people will also help us to understand the relatively simple horse.

How your expectations influence your performance

Think about all the different points of view being experienced in this illustration. Being able to see things from other people's or an animal's perspectives is a very useful tool to develop.

Exercise 30: Horseplay

Start by carefully observing your horse's habits in given situations, especially those in which you are having difficulties at the moment. Now go into second position. Imagine being your horse and decipher the signals that you are receiving. Analysis of these signals strictly from the horse's viewpoint will give an indication of the ways in which you need to adjust your behaviour.

Now imagine what it is like to be the horse in the following scenario.

The rider...	**And as the horse receives it** (with some anthropomorphic comments for fun!)
Olly, hello my beauty, how are you then?' (Friendly slap on the neck, rushes off.)	'Olly, words words words.' (Olly thinks 'Ouch - oh, does that mean a tit-bit? Aww... Nothing.')
'Hey, Olly aren't you excited, we're off to a show now. You can have your hay after I've spruced you up a bit when we're on the road.' (Hurried grooming session.) 'Stop that, ... come on pick up your feet, ... don't you dare bite me...'	'Words words Olly words words words.' (Olly thinks 'She's a bit tense about something, I wonder what? Ohh, why does she use the brush so hard where I'm a bit muddy AND sensitive. Not nearly enough nice work with the bodybrush. VERY painful pulling of things from my mane. How was I supposed to know that meant pick up my feet? Well I FANCIED a quick nip in the circumstances. Where's my grub?')
'Come on Olly, into the box, walk on now, ... stop it, ... you are going in, ... come on get IN. Right... you ARE going in... (Usual loading scenes, pushing and pulling, ropes and all, ending with a slap and leaving a bit late, so driving a bit faster...)	'Words words words, Olly words words words.' (Olly thinks 'I would go in if I could see inside properly, it's so dark and it rocks when I stand on the ramp; it doesn't feel very stable to me. Why are they getting so upset, perhaps it means something dangerous is happening and I'd better get ready to run. Ouch. Slam. Oh, it's gone dark...')

Then an endless journey ensues, the horse is in the dark and alone, gravity is absent on every corner, and there are sudden lurches and stops. If you were the horse would you go in the box next time?

Tips to cope with a spooky horse

1 **Step into the mentality of your horse.** Can you identify and understand his reason for spooking?

- Is it because that paper bag genuinely surprised him?
- Is he highly alert because it is a windy day and the sounds and smells are travelling in from afar?
- Or is it his idea of fun because he's feeling great?
- Where there is pain or discomfort the horse may look for distractions as an excuse to run away. The chances of him just being `naughty´ for the sake of it are remote – that is a human way of thinking.
- Is he picking up tension from you and going into an exaggerated response, too?

2 **Check out your own response** – each of these scenarios should bring a different reaction from you.

- If the spook was from genuine surprise, then it can be accepted, acknowledged and a sense of `it's OK, it's nothing´ sent to the horse.
- On a windy day increase the level of calmness with which you ride – or choose not to ride out but stay in an enclosed area, depending on your ability to relax.
- When it's your horse's idea of fun, find a way of gently, but firmly, telling him it is not acceptable –

maybe a halt and `no´. Immediately after make sure you forgive and forget so that you maintain the association with the behaviour rather than with being ridden.

- Where there is a possibility of pain or discomfort, do whatever you can to remedy it – would you put up with being ridden if it hurt you? Recently I heard of a young horse that spooked and bucked off his rider. It turned out that the horse's back was so badly bruised from an ill-fitting saddle that he just responded to the pressure. Wouldn't you?
- When your tension is creating his, then work on it through the exercises in this book. See particularly anchoring, p.86.

3 **Think long-term** – if your horse is the sensitive type or has a great deal of tension around him, he is likely to respond more quickly, and spook more, than a phlegmatic horse. If you are nervous then you will add to his tension. Seek professional help to clear the reasons for the tension in both you and your horse. And be aware that you might be incompatible and there might be a point when it is better for you to part ways than risk accidents.

Case study: A problem solved through second positioning

A conflict arose at a livery yard between Sophie, who owned Piper, and Angela the yard manager. Sophie thought Piper was not getting enough turn-out, but Angela was adamant she didn't want to stay out longer.

Piper was on her own as Sophie didn't want her turned out with other horses, and she simply paced the fence.

When we met, Sophie was thinking of moving yards. The problem only came up in casual conversation, although it was obviously upsetting her a lot. **We used second positioning to understand the situation from Angela's point of view.** Through this, Sophie realised the amount of knowledge and responsibility Angela had, how she was worried that she might lose a client, but that she felt that Piper was just fretting and

churning up the fields and could end up getting hurt. **Then Sophie stepped into Piper's shoes, and realised that the situation was stressing the horse, too.** She decided turn her out with an older gelding, and she asked Angela to monitor the situation and do what she felt was best.

With another horse as company, Piper was happy being out for longer. Through this compromise, everyone was happier.

Exercise 31: Perceptual positions and logical levels

It is helpful to go through these steps with a friend or guide who can keep you on track, in particular making sure that you associate fully into each role.

1 Imagine a situation where you need some insights into other people – or your horse. Mark the three positions – first, second and third – on the floor using pieces of paper.

2 Step into first position, being yourself in that situation. Make a note of what you see hear and feel, your posture, how you are behaving, what skills you have and don't have, what your main beliefs are – and what your identity and 'mission' is in this situation (see logical levels, p.46).

3 Step out and shake this off.

4 Step into third position and look objectively at the situation, as if you were the world's expert in it, or a really excellent diplomat. Make sure that you verbalise in this role, using the two participant's first names, not 'I', 'she', 'he'. What can you say about how the person with your name is behaving? How they are motivated? Consider the other person or the horse from this perspective – as the wise old thing, what do you notice?

5 Step into second position, taking time to think about body posture, gestures, speed of speaking, any colloquial expressions used, their skills and capabilities, what they would have to believe to have those behaviours and skills. Talk about the situation from their perspective.

6 Move between the positions, making sure that you go into third position before each time that you go between first and second. You will gain sufficient insight to identify some new understanding and alternative behaviour for you to take into first position.

This exercise is used to develop an understanding of the other person, so that you can be more flexible in your response to their behaviour. Remember you can't actually change the person. See also logical levels (p.46), associated/disassociated (p.69), positive intent (p.60) and modelling (p.104).

Rapport and listening skills

Building rapport and having the ability to communicate effectively with others to build trust and understanding is a vital part of developing relationships. These may be instructor/pupil, examiner/candidate, selector/rider or simply friend/friend. Part of a good rapport is the ability to see someone else's viewpoint, even if they can't see yours.

Exercise 32:
Circle of friends

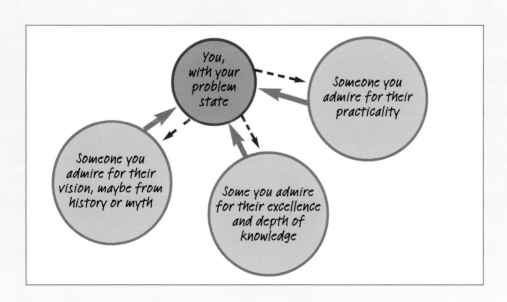

This exercise invokes the power of the different perceptual positions (p.96), which each involve a different meta-programme (p.32), and it also uses spatial anchoring – in fact, it is several processes wrapped up in one!

1 Choose an area where you will be able to mark out four different circles, each one stride from a middle point. You could put a marker down so that you remember where to stand for each.

2 Think about a situation where you feel unmotivated, perhaps, or have lost your focus. Stand in the circle that will represent this situation. Recall what it is like, seeing what you see, hearing what you hear and feeling what you feel.

3 Now choose someone that you admire for their practicality, someone you know quite well. Step into their circle and imagine being them – stand how they would stand, take on their gestures and phraseology. Look over at where you were standing and, from this second position, give that 'other you' some advice.

4 Return to your original circle and receive the advice – notice the difference it makes to your perception.

5 Repeat step 3 using someone you admire for their excellence – someone who can do the 'something' you need, better than you can. Remember to step back into your original circle to receive the advice.

6 Finally, think about someone who is detached from the situation – a visionary with great wisdom. It may be someone from history or even mythology. Step into their circle and send yourself a piece of advice, then step into the original circle to receive it.

7 From the original circle, take a moment to look at each 'friend' and thank them for their advice, then look to the future and consider what you have learnt from them and how you will behave differently now. You will have a different posture and physical attitude as you think about it, too.

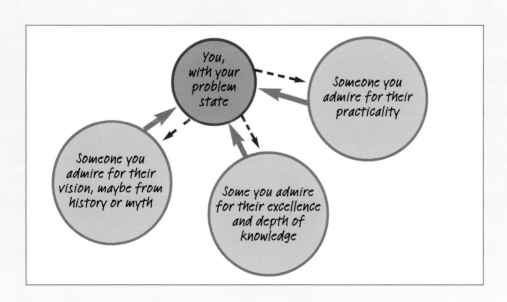

Case study:
Anne can do it!

Anne found that although she was riding her horse happily enough, whenever there came a little problem in her schooling, she tended to back off and leave it for another day. She wanted to have more tenacity and confidence to ride through the situation and enjoy the sense of improving the horse more.

Stacked anchors (p.88) for tenacity and confidence could help, however, we used the circle of friends exercise to give an even stronger resource. In her start position, Anne went back to a memory of what it felt like at a bad schooling session. She was in a defeatist frame of mind, saying things like, 'Oh, I can't be bothered, it won't work today, I haven't got the energy, I can't ride.' Her stance looked fed up: head down, shoulders rounded, no eye contact.

Her first advisor was her brother. She stepped into a space imagining being him, looking at 'useless Anne'. **His advice was, 'Go out and do it, you're strong, you can do it.'** When she stepped back into being Anne to receive this advice, she saw an image of them both cycling up hill, it was like being on a path, a journey. She thanked him.

Her next advisor was Bill, a rider and trainer she admired. **When she stepped into Bill's space and imagined being him, his advice was to say 'Give it a go, it's fun to work through things; you'll feel better when you get an improvement.'** Anne thought about these words and what it would be like, then, when she stepped into the useless Anne space to receive this advice, she heard the song with the words 'You've got to search for the hero inside yourself' and saw herself cantering in balance. She thanked Bill.

Anne's third advisor – a personality from history – was Gandhi. When she stepped into his space, she felt very determined, but with no aggression. He was very sure of himself – he was his own mentor. **Gandhi's advice to her was 'You've got the resources within you; it's all within you.'** Stepping into her original place and receiving this powerful advice made Anne feel very positive, and she thanked him.

The Anne at the end of the exercise looked so different from the one of just a few minutes earlier. She was standing more upright, looking up and around confidently, smiling – we had achieved the feeling. When we imagined a future schooling session, she was enjoying the progressive nature of the work, looking for little bits of improvement, determined to finish on a good note, in a lovely happy harmony with her horse.

A few months later she commented that she was amazed at how she could now trust her instincts much more and was able to ride without feeling nervous. She added that she still found the words of her advisors and the song came back to her as she rode!

Learning from excellent riders 12

As I always found instruction interesting I never had an attitude problem about doing what I was told. I also learned a lot from watching the riders I admired. It didn't matter what they were doing – racing, polo or whatever it was. If I thought they were good, I tried to analyse why and copy them. I copied Pop initially as he rode one handed around the farm, more like a cowboy than anything else, I learned to sit on a bucking horse, arguably better than he could! from 'So Far, So Good' by Mark Todd.

How do they do it?

'All human beings share the same neurology.
What is possible for one is possible for anyone.'*

When a top rider is asked how he or she does something, they often will answer 'I don't know' or 'I just do it'. Through being repeated over a long period, **their ability has become unconscious and they don't know how they do it.** This also indicates why **someone who is a brilliant rider may not be able to teach others** to ride as well as they can.

The learning cycle (see pp.26–27) ensures that as a skill is accomplished, it becomes a unconscious process, and the more it is practised, the deeper it is installed. Think back to your first driving lesson, trying to co-ordinate clutch, gear lever and accelerator, and still having to steer and look where you were going. Yet now you can do these things, perhaps even at the same time as finding your way, unwrapping sweets, tuning the radio and even having a 'phone conversation. That is how easily a skill becomes unconscious and natural to us.

One of the core principles of NLP is that if someone else can do something, then so can you. This does not literally mean you can become exactly like someone else (NLP does not help you grow longer legs or change sex!), it is about starting to recognise and take on the attitudes and beliefs of other people – 'those who can'. This is because any ability to do something is made up of a series of skills, woven together and including the attitudes and beliefs that are the unconscious aspects of their performance, as well as their visible behaviours. Called modelling, the study of the unconscious strategies and beliefs of an excellent performer is at the heart of NLP.

What is modelling?

The modelling process consists of close questioning of the person who has the skill and listening for the sub modalities, linguistic patterns and beliefs that come out in the subsequent conversation. (See pp.72-73 for examples of Mark Todd's language patterns.) Also by observing subtle behavioural signals when the person is performing the skill, and asking about it, you can reveal the detailed structure of the skill. The process of unravelling the skill gives the person being modelled great insight into their unconscious behaviour – they really enjoy the experience. When three or four people who are experts at the skill are compared, certain key patterns emerge and these are used to construct the final 'model' that is common to those who demonstrate the ability.

As Mark Todd's words on page 103 illustrate, modelling is something we do at some level all the time. It is one of the reasons why a good instructor will have such an influence on you – you take on their beliefs and attitudes as you learn from them.

Think about a brilliant rider in isolation from the horses they ride – after all they can get similar results from many different horses. You will realise their skill is as much about determination, confidence and positive attitude as it is about balance, suppleness and technical ability. These are all resourceful states (see p.86). In fact, their physical shape, fitness and athleticism are a reflection of these attitudes. The best riders are slim and fit because that fits with their belief system about riding well.

Modelling is a very powerful process, because once you understand exactly how someone does

*NLP Presupposition

something well, it is possible to learn the sequence they use. Think how much your riding would improve if you were to take on the same beliefs, attitudes and level of confidence as your riding hero.

Modelling is also used in changing a limiting behaviour (see p.42–43 and ch.13), because once you understand why you are responding in a certain way, you can address the reason and change it!

How to use these models

The following pages contain models of how 'those that can' do what they do well.

• Most of the models are made up from interviews with three to five people. The model may also be supported by the writings and observation of that person and his or her ability.

• The models have been selected for what I consider is a good demonstration of the ability – this means that they have been through my filter system too! I have chosen people who are not only impressive in terms of their results, but who are also compassionate and loving with their horses.

• The common features of each aspect of the skill are extracted and the 'model' is developed from these. This means that idiosyncrasies have been left out – so if one brilliant competitor always mounts from the offside before riding into the ring but none of the others do, it is not a relevant fact. This makes the model as transferable as possible.

• The models consist of different aspects that tie in to the logical levels (see p.46) – environmental considerations, observable behaviour, skills and capabilities, beliefs and identity. For instance, the teachers all put emphasis on noting the safety aspects of the environment, such as likely distractions and the mood of the horse and rider, before they teach. The horse trainers all sit in a very quiet, balanced and relaxed way on their horses. The riders doing a dressage test each run the film of themselves doing the test viewed from the judge's perspective, the competition riders each believe that

it's okay to show off their achievements. In understanding how someone does something, each of the logical levels is important as they all interrelate.

• While you read these models, notice both what you currently can do and also what you don't. Try on the different elements of their patterns: imagine you are like them, with their beliefs, emotions and behaviours. Notice how or where what you currently do is different: it may that you have different beliefs; it may be that you have not developed the skills or capabilities yet; it may be that your emotional state is different. The closer you can get to the model, the closer you will be to gaining the results that they do. Identify any gaps or differences – once you have used the models to diagnose where you need to develop, you have an action plan to work to. For example, it may be that when you compare what you do with your sub modalities, you are running small, dull pictures, not huge, bright, moving ones. What would happen if you added your instructor's voice in your imagination as you visualise riding a test? Set up anchors (p.87) for more resourceful states to use when riding.

• When you have read through the models re-examine any limiting beliefs (p.43) that have come up and work on them. Maybe you realise that although you share some of the expert's beliefs, there are some that you are not yet able to take on. For instance, you know what to do to train a horse, but maybe you don't believe that a little upset can be corrected or doesn't matter, and so your performance spirals downwards with one mistake.

How those that can…
train a horse under saddle

The following is a model of different **trainers who are effective at schooling** a horse under saddle. They were selected for their success at **producing confident, safe horses** for a range of riders. Read it and compare their behaviours, attitudes and beliefs with how you think and feel when you are schooling.

These riders defined training a horse under saddle as **working together softly and easily, allowing the horse to develop new skills** with comfort and consistency. For them, it is important that **the horse is enjoying itself** in a relaxed state, expressing itself. It is responsive and working with the trainer because it has confidence in him or her. As a result, both horse and rider would be having a safe and happy time, **building a relationship and learning together**.

What they do – conscious and unconscious strategies

1	**Get the horse into a relaxed state.**	By being relaxed themselves. This involves mainly walking on a long rein or trotting the horse if the horse is a bit flighty.
2	**Repeat previous training exercises.**	Once settled, they start putting the horse through previous training exercises and making transitions. They reinforce good behaviour through small acknowledgements – pats and words, or breaks in the work.
3	**Run a movie in their mind of how they want the horse to be.**	This is in the future – it may be long-term in a year or so, or short-term. The picture is disassociated – it is of them both working together, maybe at a show or schooling. It is very large (maybe as big as a cinema screen), in full colour and moving. It shows short clips relevant to what they are doing or want to be doing – for example, a balanced and a soft transition, or an engaged canter on a straight line.
4	**See how the horse currently looks.**	They imagine a movie of how the horse is going, particularly the overall outline, compared to the first movie. They notice what will make the biggest difference in bringing the two pictures closer together.
5	**Continually check themselves against the two movies.**	They compare the movies and make little adjustments as necessary. They are putting everything in place so the horse can succeed. They may be improving their own balance, increasing the aid, softening the contact – whatever is necessary. They repeat certain movements and exercises, changing every so often so that the horse does not anticipate a pattern.
6	**Are aware of the horse's responses.**	They look out for the horse's responses and assess whether they are moving towards their goal. When they notice that they are, they acknowledge it through a kind word, softer rein contact, stroking or giving the horse a rest.

Beliefs

- The trainers all have a sense of liking the personality and temperament of the horse they are training, and feel drawn to it – they want to develop this horse.
- They believe you get the best out of the horse through being relaxed, consistent and encouraging.
- They believe that training the horse is a privileged partnership giving them a real sense of harmony and satisfaction – sometimes it is bliss or euphoria! Each time they ride the horse, they see themselves as developing the relationship – they believe horses are better as partners than servants.
- At a deeper belief level, they feel humbled by the horse, for what it is offering them.

- They believe training is a progressive and gentle game. It usually starts from a different place each time. One day the horse may be spooky, one day attentive, one day tense. This does not matter. They know that some days they will start two or three steps back. Again, this did not matter; their aim is to get back to the end point of the previous lesson and then, ideally, add another learning skill.
- They believe it is important to 'let go' when either they or the horse make a mistake – it doesn't matter in the long term.
- They know their own capability as a rider/trainer. They would not claim to be able to train a horse beyond their current level, or one that was too big or too small for them. From this they know that they can deal with anything the horse may throw at them.

How they cope when things go wrong

- If the horse fails on one exercise or movement, they do another exercise or give the horse a break then come back to it. Sometimes they decide to leave training for now and try another day.
- As well as running the film discussed in step 4 (p.106), they add a voice command — telling themselves how to reinforce their behaviour.
- They are aware of where the horse's attention is and its state of mind. If it is tense internally, they take their attention off its behaviour and focus on relaxing their own personal state. Where a horse is tense externally — such as 'looking for spooks for fun' — they use stronger aids and maybe a voice reprimand to get its attention back to them as rider.

How they feel

The riders are confident and open to the horse and what they will both learn that day. They really enjoy their riding. They operate in the moment, very calmly and with a sense of being in touch with the horse and its spiritual nature. This is an internal, concentrated focus, although they also keep a 'lifeline' of awareness of what else is happening around them.

What you would particularly see and hear

- A balanced position — legs and hands as still and soft as possible.
- A kind, quiet voice.
- The rider staying calm and confident no matter what the horse does.
- The rider quickly overcoming any setback or forgiving any disobedience from the horse.

Their knowledge and capabilities

- They understand the psychology of a horse — that it is a flight animal and that it will follow a leader.
- They have realistic expectations of the horse's capability — they know what is required for the task the horse is to do and what to look for in terms of conformation and temperament.
- They have an understanding of how a horse moves and what is easy or difficult for it.

Training or educating?

J. Allen Boone in *Kinship with All Life* highlighted the difference between training an animal and educating one.

'The significant difference lies in whether one places emphasis on the mental or physical part of the animal. The conventional trainer starts from the negative premise that he is dealing with a dumb and inferior form of life with a limited brain capacity. As long as the animal looks its best and obeys orders promptly, he is satisfied. With its thinking and natural impulses walled off with this method, it becomes a four-legged slave, submissively serving the moods and whims of the human ego.'

'The animal educator does the reverse of this. He places full emphasis on the mental rather than the physical part of the animal. He knows that its appearance, actions and accomplishments are only the outward expressions of its state of mind. He seeks to help the animal make use of its thinking faculties so that there will be corresponding results in its looks, character and actions.'

How those that can…
ride a dressage test

One successful young international rider who I modelled had **a fascinating unconscious strategy for riding her tests accurately and fluently,** which has been validated by modelling other riders and trainers. This model explains this strategy as a demonstration of **how valuable it can be to understand second positioning (p.96) and sub modalities (p.68–69).** (For the attitudes and beliefs of competitive riders see p.112.)

What she does – conscious and unconscious strategies

1	**She imagines what she and the horse look like.**	The view is from the side or front as they ride the test – this is how they are seen by the judges. This imagined picture is panoramic, full size, full colour and moving at actual speed.
2	**She runs the film five or six strides into the future.**	She is imagining what the horse will be looking like then. She is creating her film from the feelings she is getting from the horse and her knowlege of what movements will be coming up next.
3	**She takes action to correct the horse.**	She has a close up box in the top lefthand side of her imagined screen. In it there is a close-up of leg or hand or position, that shows her what to do to improve the picture further. As the feeling from the horse changes, or the knowledge of the next part of the test comes in, so this close-up picture changes to tell her how to respond. If in her main picture the horse was a bit hollow or starting to come against the hand, for example, the zoom would indicate more leg or a tweak of the rein or whatever she needs to do to correct it. Because the film is running in the future, she has time to make the changes necessary and see how they affect the next movement or sequence. As a result, she is always making the adjustments before the balance has deteriorated or the outline has changed, and so she is able to ride really polished tests.

It is interesting that it was only when we talked and revealed the strategy through careful questions that the dressage rider became aware of what she did. Once she understood her strategy, she was able to add the voice of her trainer giving constructive suggestions in her imagination, too. Having identified her strategy and improved it, we could then leave it to return to being an unconscious skill, which is how it works best.

Watch a dressage or show-jumping class for a while and you will see how it is possible to predict what will happen – you can see the horse losing balance on the turn and because of that, his head will come up or he will run out at the next fence. This rider's strategy allowed her to pick up this information and do something about it before the outside world would notice anything going wrong. Notice its similarities with the jumping model (p.114). Then think how this information could help you if you were riding a test or jumping a round.

Remember the test!

British international rider Richard Davison (*below*) explains his method for learning a new dressage test and overcoming any fear of forgetting the test

'When studying a new test on paper, I try to imagine blocks of movement in my head. It might be an extended trot sandwiched between two half passes or the flying changes with the canter pirouette in between. In the final test of my study, to ensure that I really know where I am going, I imagine the mental block situation. This occurs when we have been concentrating on the way of going of the horse, have failed to prepare for the next movement and have a complete blank as to what to do next. It happens to the best of us and it is therefore necessary to address it rather than avoid confronting the situation. I overcome this problem by ensuring that if I were to stick a pin into any part of the test sheet I would immediately be able to state the next movements.'

How those that can…
enjoy competing

This model has evolved from a range of modelling **interviews with people who love to compete**. Most of them are riders with disabilities who compete in open competitions. It is very humbling and inspiring to consider their achievements. Some common themes – especially those surrounding beliefs – emerged. The model is likely to be **particularly beneficial for those who feel stressed even at the thought of going to a show!** Chances are that negative beliefs about competing were formed in younger days. Having to stand up in front of the class and perform often puts people off similar exposure for life.

Capabilities and beliefs

- There is a consistent desire among the models with disabilities to get on in life, to better themselves – never just to sit back and let life happen. This self-knowledge drives them to want to be the best – and stay there. Another belief tied into this is the need to be proactive: 'you've got to work for it and make your success happen.'

- At a higher logical level, there is a spiritual belief that the example they give to others will inspire those people to do more with their lives.

- The riders with disabilities actively enjoy being different; they don't want to be 'normal'. After all, throughout their lives, they have been noticed. Through competing, they are acknowledged, so that in a way they become 'famous'. Being noticed gives them confidence.

- A simple but consistent capability or belief of this group is the desire to be watched and applauded: 'Look at me!' There is a great pride in their own personal achievement and that of the horse. It is also important to them that the horse is relaxed and enjoying the experience with them.

- In the professional riders I interviewed, this desire to be watched has developed into showmanship – a love of entertaining and being in the spotlight. For instance, for Jenny Loriston-Clark, an upbringing as a show pony rider set her in excellent stead for international dressage. The show jumpers I modelled also had a particular enjoyment of the personality, drama and spectacle of horses jumping in an international ring.

How they feel

Meeting any of these models you would be struck by how much pleasure they get from riding in front of an audience. Their faces light up and they become more animated at the thought of it. The descriptions are of getting a great buzz, an incredible, happy, invincible feeling. It is very empowering and boosts them in other areas of their lives. Imagine this happening for you before a show – how much more enjoyable would competing be?

Tips to enjoy competing

You've read the schedule, booked the date in your diary and sent off the cheque. Now, how do you feel? Worried and nervous? Or relaxed and confident that you will enjoy the day? Considering that most people ride for pleasure, why do so many dread competing?

- Ask yourself why you are doing it and decide on what you want from the show: it may be to be with friends, have a new experience, to enjoy the day or to win a rosette. By clarifying your goals, you can then focus on what you need to do to achieve them (see the outcome process p.14)
- Talk to your friends and instructor about what to expect and what to do. Go and watch a show. Get plenty of detail, so you can imagine doing it yourself, step-by-step. Then visualise what it will be like, from preparing the day before, packing the vehicle, driving there, arriving in plenty of time, sorting out where to go and when you need to be ready and mounted. See yourself riding calmly and confidently, enjoying your horse and the whole experience, smiling and laughing. Imagine what you will be saying at different moments and how you will feel. Try out the visualisation with the same happy scenes whether there is sunshine, wind or rain (see exercise 25, p.84).

- Imagine the point of view of the judge or course builder – how they want to get a fair result, help the competitors, even to be invited back to judge again. It can be helpful to think of times when you have been in a situation that is similar to theirs, maybe at work or with your family. By thinking through from this perspective, you can look at your standards more objectively and get some insights into what else you can do to get a good result. And, when you imagine being an organiser, notice how nice it would be to be thanked at the end of the day! (See perceptual positioning p.96.)

- Finally, remember that the person you are competing against and proving most to is yourself. It's your day – you chose to enter, now choose to get the best experiences you can from it.

How those that can…

love jumping

Jumping seems to be something riders either love and do with a passion or avoid like the plague. Where there is any element of tension in the rider's mind about jumping, this will be magnified in their behaviour and then by the horse.

When talking to the confident jumping riders, the first phrase that came across consistently was the need to see or feel a stride to the fence. 'If you can see the stride it will be heaven, if not it could be hell!' This is the red herring that so often catches out novice riders. They focus on 'trying to see a stride' – but what on earth does this mean? It is a phrase that describes a complex interaction of feelings and visual images. It is not just a question of looking at a take-off point, it is about feeling the horse's rhythm, speed and impulsion and being able to correct it. Without an understanding of it, jumping becomes a hit or miss affair – nerve-racking for horse and rider.

Understanding jumping

To understand how to jump, and with it how to see a stride, it is useful to know how the horse jumps, and the importance of developing the canter to understand the feeling of speed, stride length and impulsion. The jumping riders I talked to all emphasised the importance of the horse being forward and in balance when jumping: in turn, this gives rhythm. Good rhythm means the horse has the ability to lengthen and shorten its stride easily. And then you can see a stride.

At lower level competitions, say up to 1.10m, the

FORWARD + BALANCE = RHYTHM = CAN ADJUST STRIDE = CAN JUMP FENCE

horse should be able to adjust his own stride length on the approach to the fence to jump it well. For the horse to be able to do this, the rider needs to stay out of its way, in balance and riding to a constant rhythm. In fact, the less the rider does, the better, especially at these lower heights. The rider's role is simply to follow the movement – in particular the arms should allow the neck to be free so that the back can jump in a supple way. A soft arm is, therefore, one of the keys to seeing a stride. Cross-country courses are often built on uneven terrain and, therefore, stride length will vary much more and the rider will have even less influence. This is why it is important that the cross-country horse is allowed to judge its own take-off point and adapt to the terrain itself. Jumps up and down hill are a good test of both the horse's and rider's balance.

Capabilities and beliefs

- When the jumpers work a horse in canter and trot there is emphasis on the horse being 'off the leg', responsive to the lightest leg aid to go forward, and weight or rein aid to slow. Schooling involves plenty of transitions within the pace. There is also a need to keep the horse relaxed about jumping, so that it is forward, yet still calm. This is the rider's responsibility. And one of the beliefs around this is that the riders see jumping as no big deal: 'it is only an elevated canter stride'. But these riders do not ask the horses to jump higher than they are relaxed to jump. Until the horse can gain a number of double clears at one height, they do not progress to the next height – and so the horse builds in confidence and ability.

- The jumpers believe there is always a stride and that, even if you do not see it immediately, you can pick one up. This comes back to being able to lengthen and shorten the stride easily. If you want to improve your jumping, work on your awareness of impulsion, balance and rhythm in canter. If you were only to jump a fence when the canter is right, you would make many more good jumps to build your confidence with.

- One point is the difference in speed of show jumping compared to dressage and hacking, and, of course, cross country is that much faster again. Novice show-jumping courses are designed to be ridden at 325 metres per minute (mpm), while an international trial will be at 400mpm. However, novice cross-country events are 520m per minute, while the advanced course in a 3-day event is ridden at 570mpm and the steeplechase

at 690mpm. All these are faster than the fastest movement in a dressage test – a lengthened canter down one long side. So one of the other notable points in the models was their confidence in riding at a higher speed. This ties in with their much reduced need to 'be in control' than those riders who choose not to jump. The jumpers are still 'in control', but they are relaxed with being at a faster speed, and there is a calm boldness about their riding. A buck and a skip from a horse doesn't worry them at all. They believe 'it's just what horses do' and 'a horse that can buck can jump'.

What they do – conscious and unconscious strategies

Just as in the dressage rider's model, the jumpers see themselves in a large, disassociated film that is in full, bright colour. The key sub modality is that the film changes speed, coming to slow-motion at each fence, so they can see themselves and the horse effortlessly jumping over.

What you would see

The confidence good jumping riders exhibit comes in part from security of position: a secure lower leg that barely moves throughout the jump and over which the body pivots. This provides a base for the rider to balance on. After all, if the rider is not in balance on the horse, the horse cannot be expected to jump well – how would you cope with a loose and heavy rucksack swinging around on your back as you jumped?

Another point to note is that good jumping riders are very still and yet relaxed and soft in the seat – meaning the thighs, pelvis and lower back – in all paces and when jumping. The phrase 'let the jump come to you' relates to this. The overall impression is of relaxed ease, with the body able to follow the horse softly and absorb the thrust of take-off and impact of landing. On the approach to the fence, they will be riding the canter forward, ensuring that the impulsion and balance is correct and maintained. In comparison, a novice or nervous jumper will often tense their body, especially the thighs and pelvis, and accelerate in the last few paces. This changes the horse's balance and puts it on the forehand, from where the jump will be less fluent.

You will also notice good jumpers sitting up and looking for the fence well ahead of turns. The head, being such a heavy part of the body, is critical to balance. And when the head is up, the rider cannot get in front of the movement, whether they jump with an upright or light jumping seat.

How it goes wrong

Often novice riders don't ride truly forwards into a contact, in fact, they often misinterpret 'riding forward to a fence' as 'accelerate to it'. This is worsened by a focus on being on the bit, rather than allowing a natural head position. Imagine the common picture of the horse being ridden on a tight rein to the show jump, thus held back, it cannot be forward, which it needs to do in order to jump. No wonder the horse starts to fight for its head and get faster, and so a vicious circle is set up.

Where a horse needs speed to jump – whether due to tension or lack of impulsion – it will lose balance and rhythm and thus cannot easily adjust its stride for itself. Therefore, it will put in long strides or get underneath the fence, so the rider tries to control more, riding with a restricted rein and then suddenly releasing, dropping the horse and changing the balance just in front of the fence, causing a fault or a stop.

Imagine you are a horse, wanting to jump but every time you do so, finding that the rider moves on take-off, disrupting your movement, or lands in a heap on your neck after each fence. Or there are straps on your head so you can't use your natural ability to balance. How long would you keep trying for your rider?

Tips to improve your jumping

- Work on confidence with riding at higher speeds and 'letting go' of the need to be in control.
- Build your understanding of how the horse jumps, and the importance and interrelation of speed, balance and rhythm – good jumpers feel these and can correct the horse quickly and almost imperceptibly thus 'seeing a stride'.
- Develop an independent position that can change with the horse's constant adjustments of balance.
- Improve your leg position to make it more secure.
- Have relaxed arms that allow and follow the movement of the horse's neck.
- Maintain a soft and still yet following seat and thighs.
- Keep your head up, looking for the next fence
- Visualise jumping the fence in slow-motion.

How those that can…
think natural horsemanship

Recently, there has been a substantial increase in awareness of and interest in natural horsemanship, with American trainers such as **Monty Roberts, Pat Parelli and Mark Rashid** promoting the approach. **This style of horsemanship has its background in western riding**, and although western tack is not essential to ride and train your horse in these methods, enthusiasts commonly use the equipment.

Although there are some specific strategies, the main feature of the model is the strength of the beliefs from which natural horsemen operate.

Is it a better way?

Natural horsemanship has been adopted as a branch of holistic riding. However, it should be noted that in its cowboy heritage, horses were very much working animals. In the teaching there is little emphasis on awareness of the veterinary aspects of health, fitness and physiology, nor tack fitting, nor the riders position and how these all interrelate to the horse's soundness and ability to perform the tasks required. For a less accomplished rider, these all need to be a focus of further awareness and learning. Some of the teaching is highly procedural – almost dogmatic – and this may not interest people wanting to extend their learning across different equestrian fields. And, in the wrong hands, a thin rope halter can be more severe than a mild snaffle bit.

What they do – conscious and unconscious strategies

Set the horse up for success so that he is able to understand what is required of him. This is the overall objective. Parelli particularly promotes step-by-step exercises. Part of these are his seven games, which he describes as the games horses play with each other. The horse will perform the tasks when the handler can cause their idea to become the horse's own, demonstrating a feeling and understanding of him. He looks to control through communication, using increasing phases of pressure until the horse responds. They are very quick to reward the horse with a nut or a rest.

Natural horsemen **second position (see p.96) the horse extensively**. 'Think what he is thinking, see what he is seeing, feel what he is feeling.' By becoming as much like their horse as possible, they gain an understanding of what it will take to reassure and motivate him. A great deal of this is done on the ground, observing the horse's reactions and teaching him to respond, before asking for the same under saddle.

Beliefs

- All the natural horsemen modelled share an almost spiritual regard for the horse; a belief that horses are our teachers and that we can learn from them on an on-going journey together.
- The other consistently held belief is that the rider wants to form a partnership – indeed will be privileged if the horse will allow it. Unlike many other schools of horsemanship, there is no contest or battle of will in their map of the relationship, no suggestion of making the horse do what the handler wants. Instead, the focus is on the handler behaving so the horse can respect them – a respect that is hard to get and easy to lose. This entails a responsibility to be entirely consistent in their dealings with the horse.
- Natural horsemen also adopt a number of beliefs about horses. For instance, that they want safety, comfort and play, rather than praise and recognition.

How they cope when things to wrong

- Whenever the horse does not respond as expected, the handler will go back through all the steps – and there could be several – until they identify where the misunderstanding took place – where they as handler have behaved inconsistently. This on-going analysis provides pleasure in itself as the depth of knowledge and understanding and relationship is continually increasing.
- The thought of the relationship with the horse and the knowledge they are gaining is a strong motivator in the down times. They believe that you can learn from your mistakes.

How they feel

Natural horsemen report a strong emotional relationship with their horses and with it a tremendous feeling of satisfaction and sense of achievement when the relationship is demonstrated.

What you would see and hear

Quietness and consistency in the way the horses are handled.

Good natural horsemen simply do not lose their temper or become tense with the horse. Their ability to control their emotional state is excellent – something that any rider should aspire to.

Their knowledge and capabilities

Apart from this emotional control, natural horsemanship emphasises an understanding of the horse's natural response, how horses think and act and the importance of the herd influence (see Know Your Horse, p.92).

Note

Natural horsemanship 'gurus' recommend colder-blooded, fairly passive and less dominant horses for their followers to learn their systems with. This is a safety driven policy since an alert young Thoroughbred will have a speed of response and range of movement that could be very testing for a novice rider. Most consider the typical cowboy horse or quarter horse, with its smaller size and calm temperament, yet agility and speed, as their ideal.

Case study: The philosophy of the original horsemen

The love and relationship with the horse is not new or unique to natural horsemanship – consider the 'cowboys and Indians' and their horses, or in Britain, perhaps the relationship of the 'gentleman with his hunters'.

Xenophon was among the first to promote the psychological aspects of equitation, and how it can increase the understanding of riding in general. Take to heart Xenophon's instructions: 'Never should you treat your horse in anger, for there is something blind in anger which makes us commit actions that later will be regretted.' He follows this with another insight: **'Anything forced or misunderstood can never be beautiful.** If a dancer were forced to dance by whips and spurs, he would be no more beautiful than a horse trained under similar conditions.'

In the 1940s J. Allen Boone interviewed one of the original great Indian chiefs to find out how Indians could ride and be so at one with their mounts. The insights he gained were that to 'full know' you need to grow up with the Indian pony as your brother. The essence was the interrelating of all their interests – the Indian relied on the horse and the horse on the Indian (for food, safety and so on). **This togetherness blended into a oneness, where horse and rider function as a single unit in mind, body, heart and purpose.** This summarises the deeper level of relationship sought by Natural Horsemanship leaders. The best relationships between huntsmen or competitors and their horses could be considered similar.

Boone also explored the Bedouin tribesman's relationship with their horses. **Their success lay basically in the fine quality of their thinking about their animals.** This expressed 'genuineness … sincerity … admiration … appreciation … respect … affection … a sense of fellowship in being … humility … unselfishness … sympathy … and a desire to share their best, and only their best, with their animals.' The Bedouin regarded horses as celestial creatures. When a mare was in foal, the chief would kneel on his prayer rug and read the best Oriental literature to her, meditating and praying. Just like the American Indians, they recognised animals as being on a mental and spiritual level with themselves.

This may seem a far cry from trying to get your horse to do a square halt, or mucking out before rushing to work, but the questions it raises about your relationship with your horse and the heights you want to take it to are worth pondering.

How those that can…
share their knowledge

This modelling study was undertaken with excellent dressage trainers, **instructors who were truly passionate about their teaching**. They were training up to Prix St Georges level, yet one aspect that struck me was the **equal enthusiasm and care** with which they would **teach a novice horse and rider** combination.

What they do – conscious and unconscious strategies

The models all set up their lessons in a similar way, establishing rapport through asking questions about how the rider had progressed since the last lesson and establishing an outcome for the session. The core part of the lesson runs the following repeating loop:

1	**Instructor watches the horse and rider intently.**	They concentrate fully on their pupils.
2	**They create an internal picture.**	The picture is of how they imagine the horse and rider could look and they compare this with what they see in front of them.
3	**Imagine themselves 'climbing inside the body of the rider'.**	They consider what it is like to be the rider by taking second position (see p.96). They may also imagine being the horse, giving them an insight into any resistance and crookedness.
4	**They decide what to say and then say it.**	Where the rider is experiencing difficulty understanding the command, they may add a physical or visual demonstration to show what they want to happen.
5	**Watch for the reaction of horse and rider.**	As the rider responds to the command, they continue to watch intently, again comparing their internatl picture of what they believe the combination can be like, with what is happening.
6	**Watch for the difference they want.**	When they see progress towards the improvement, they make a short positive comment like 'Yes' or 'Good'. They then go back to step 1 and repeat the process with another exercise or to improve this progress further.

By working in small but logical steps these instructors are able to help the riders put many small changes into place, and achieve a consistent improvement. This gives great insight into how there is so much more happening than just the watching and commenting that you see from the outside. No wonder it can be so tiring to teach – with all that imaginary riding!

Beliefs

The beliefs the teachers hold fall into two key categories:

- They believe they are creating something beautiful – the harmony between horse and rider, a beautiful picture of a horse proud and powerful, lightly responding to an elegant rider. 'When something improves in the horse, it will instantly look more beautiful, easier and lighter.'

- The instructors modelled also have a love of learning (see Choosing the right instructor, p.126). They sincerely believe in lifelong learning, that they will never stop learning from horse and rider. 'You never stand still, you're either improving or destroying.' Their chosen role means that they are continually enhancing their own learning as well as that of the rider and horse. 'You learn from every situation – each one opens more doors to learning more, you are fed with inspiration.'

> **NOTE**
> One instructor I explained this model to was also becoming very expert at Tai Chi. As we went through the model, she realised why she was finding it difficult to teach some riders. At the point when she imagined becoming the rider, it was so different from the free and balanced feeling that she now enjoyed in her life that it hurt her to take on their more tense and crooked positions. She went on to develop un-mounted 'body awareness' workshops for her pupils.

How they cope when things go wrong

- At all times, the instructor has an awareness of the horse's responses and external factors that may distract him. The teachers I modelled have an unspoken regard for safety and measured progression. So, when other horses are coming into the school or are playing up, for instance, they will bring their pupils to a slower pace or halt.

- Where the rider does not make the change or get the desired effect, the instructor works out another way of communicating what they want. This may involve describing it in a different way, doing a physical demonstration, riding the horse themself or drawing a diagram in the sand of the school.

- They keep running through different possibilities until the pupil can achieve the difference.

What you would see and hear

Instructors make sure:
- The pupil is watched intently throughout the lesson.
- They are dressed for the weather so they are comfortable and can concentrate on their pupils.
- All the instructors have very good voice projection, which is authoritative without being dominant.
- They use positive, constructive language, talking to the rider about the objective and solutions rather than criticising what was wrong.
- Their style tends to be options rather than procedures oriented, this gives them more flexibility in communicating ideas and coping with all the change.

Their knowledge and capabilities

They have a large repertoire of experiences to draw upon in order to come up with solutions for each situation. They have all ridden a great deal with other good instructors and have a deep and extensive knowledge of horses.

How it feels to teach well

The instructors describe the emotion and feeling they get from teaching as 'a high of some sort', 'a great buzz', 'it's great', 'it's fantastic'. They obviously get a lot of pleasure from working with their pupils.

Applying the model to teaching jumping

Although this model was developed from instructors teaching flatwork, the same process applies to teaching jumping. The instructor can see the horse's paces and attitude and imagine the horse jumping from the pace it is in.

For example, a good impulsive balanced canter looks the same in both dressage and jumping, even though the speed and length of stride may be different. When judging dressage I can look at a horse's trot or canter and see where impulsion is so lacking that horse and rider would barely be able to clear a 60cm pole – the rider needs to ask the horse to be more forward. As one top show-jumping trainer said, 'Jumping is no more than dressage with poles.' It is the rhythm, balance and straightness of the horse that will dictate the quality of the jump. In his or her mind, the instructor will see the shape of the bascule over the jump and the way in which the horse tucks its legs up, and they will use exercises accordingly to develop the jump.

Is your instructor right for you... and your horse?

- Spend time selecting the right instructor for you. It is also very important to choose someone who likes your horse – after all they will not want to imagine riding it otherwise.

- Trust your own gut feeling and intuition, rather than other people's recommendations. Just because an instructor inspires your friend it doesn't necessarily mean he or she will inspire you too, because you may be motivated differently (see pp.31–37).

- Watch other people's lessons before committing yourself to their instructor. By listening to the instructor's language and noticing their patterns, you can easily learn to spot which style they naturally use and check whether it matches yours (see p.71). Imagine you are the rider on the horse and notice how those words would work for you. Be aware of what style of teaching you respond best to and choose an instructor accordingly (see meta-programmes p.32).

- Find someone who inspires you with his or her love of learning or teaching. Simply talking or watching them will tell you this. If they look bored or make negative comments about the horse or rider they are teaching they are unlikely to truly love teaching. Remember, just because someone can ride well does not necessarily mean they can explain how they do what they do well.

- Check that their qualifications and experience suit your needs. Your instructor needs to have had sufficient experience of riding different horses and training them progressively, as well as of the techniques required to improve a movement or solve a resistance. Then they will know that what they say will really make a difference. Ask them about their experience, and who is their most influential trainer.

- A good instructor will be aware of the standard that can be achieved by you and your horse working in a steady, progressive way, rather than setting targets that are too ambitious for your horse's level of fitness or your confidence. Just because you have had an instructor for some time it doesn't mean you should always stay with them (nor that you should change instructor every time you come up against a challenge). Set your own goals for the improvement you want and notice how you are performing against these (see goal setting p.18).

- Ensure the instructor has appropriate levels of insurance to teach. Accidents can happen and a professional instructor will have a first aid qualification and professional liability insurance, usually through a national registration scheme.

- Once you have chosen an instructor you need to work frequently and openly enough together to allow their approach to take effect. Such two-way commitment allows a longer term view of the training you need, rather than a quick fix. It allows your instructor to be honest with you.

- Beware the instructor who offers to school and compete your horse for you – at a cost. This is what they are meant to be teaching you how to do.

Making flying changes 13

The significant problems we face cannot be solved at the same level of thinking we were at when we created them. Albert Einstein

Is it time for a change?

'Insanity is doing the same thing over and over…
and expecting a different result.'*

Riding is indescribably wonderful when everything is going **better and better**, but this is a sport in which, as we progress, we keep stretching the boundaries – trying more advanced moves, bigger jumps and more 'difficult' horses. That is why **falls or near misses are virtually inevitable but they don't have to be detrimental**.

I was teaching a very nervous novice rider when she fell off for the first time ever. The experience really improved her riding because she realised it was no big deal after all! She was then able to relax and get on with riding and, because of how we analysed the fall, it made her more aware of how to keep her balance.

The way we cope with riding mistakes and accidents is the real test of our ability and it is often a reflection of how we are handling 'bumps' in other areas of our life. This is why the times when it all goes wrong and you feel unable to ride to your 'old' level of ability can bring your confidence and performance down in other areas of your life, too. In many ways riding is the means by which we choose to challenge ourselves, so that we are continually learning and developing. Horses can then take on a spiritual representation of our development.

From the Bandura study (pp.28–29), it is clear that progress is not only upward. How we cope with setbacks dictates how much we grow and develop. And, thinking logically, in order to improve you will need to make changes because 'if you just did what you have always done, you would simply get what you have always got'. Indeed, if you don't change, you will find that something else will: your fear may increase, or your confidence decline.

Individual changework

NLP works with a combination of techniques that operate at the neurological level – for instance how

*Albert Einstein

you use sub modalities (see pp.68–71) – as well as challenging and adjusting beliefs (pp.42–43) through conversation and precise questions – the linguistic level. When I am working with clients, often the meetings appear to be simply conversational as we talk to identify what beliefs are in place and are causing limiting behaviour. Changework is about making a series of 'shifts' in thinking and beliefs that together add up to significant change.

All change – the knock-on effect

When you change, other people will be affected and there is likely to be a form of unconscious, subtle pressure on you to stay just as you were – otherwise your friends and family have to change, too. Suppose you previously had the equivalent of a big badge on you saying 'I'm scared of hacking/jumping/competing.' Now imagine walking into the yard without it, and acting the opposite way – with confidence, with calmness, with determination, or whatever. What would your instructor say? How would the other people in the yard respond to you? Chances are that, at one level, they preferred you as you were, because now they have to change their relationship with you! That's why, with major changes, it may sometimes be easier to make a clean break and change instructor or even yard, in order to be able to behave differently.

Using this chapter

Sometimes beliefs and habits have been part of our behaviour for so long that they become hard to shift on our own (see case study below). We become blinkered to our patterns and are not even aware of them. After all, it is much easier, on a day-to-day basis, if beliefs and habits stay in place. Then we don't need to examine our behaviour or confront whatever it is we are avoiding or notice how we are limiting ourself. So we become excellent at justifying why we do not need to change. However another 'part' of us wants to get

the pleasure that changing a belief or behaviour would bring. This is where Six-step Reframing (p.131) or conflicting belief integration (p.136) techniques are used. Using the Swish Technique (p.132) can change some habitual behaviour patterns, while the Phobia Cure (p.134) can change the way you remember the bad times and soften those negative experiences so that they no longer prevent you from riding. Sometimes you are just stuck, and a new look at the situation will help you. Use exercise 16 (p.63), exercise 32 (p.101) or exercise 37 (p.138) to help.

Case study: Rosie slows down

One of my pupils, Rosie, was a very busy rider – always fiddling with the contact and nudging her horse. She could get quite aggressive with him when he didn't respond precisely or work softly.

Needless to say, she was unable to get the results she wanted, which in this case was to ride a range of horses effectively in order to pass her professional exam – and it was becoming very frustrating and demoralizing for her.

She was surprised when I asked her about her lifestyle. **But as we talked, it became apparent that this busy-ness was reflected in virtually all areas of her life** – she had a high pressure job, young children as well as the horses, and was always on the go. She was also starting to get stress-related illnesses. From my questions, she realised that she wanted to pass the exam in order to work more from home in the long-term, doing what she loved. It would mean she slowed down a lot – deep down she knew she needed to – but how?

By talking about how this 'busy, busy' pattern was reflected in other areas of her life, she realised how her riding was a reflection of her lifestyle. Which would change first? It was a chicken and egg situation. **She decided to make her riding time her meditation time, to stop working towards the exam and simply to ride for pleasure, to**

become more aware of her body and the horse's responses – it was about creating quality time for herself. She would sometimes school and sometimes simply hack out and enjoy her horse; competing was only to be at a level that was completely within their scope, rather than trying to push for greater achievements. Our lessons were about awareness and appreciation of the horse's responses rather than surface improvement. Rosie began to really enjoy riding again, whereas before it was something that 'had' to be done, a stress she had added to her life.

> **see also:**
> *Bandura Curve*
> *pp.28–29*
> *The Value of Values*
> *pp.48–49*

Four months later a cancellation meant that Rosie took the exam, with only two week's notice – just to see what would happen and to experience the format of the day – and she passed. She was so much more relaxed in other areas of her life too – and felt healthier than ever. Her whole life had changed.

Most of these change techniques have been described step-by-step. It is helpful to be taken through the steps by a friend or a qualified NLP Master Practitioner who acts as a guide so that you can concentrate on the questions, understanding the insights and achieving the desired state.

Before you work through this chapter, it is important that you have read and understood all the earlier chapters. Many of the previous exercises will have made 'shifts' for you, since NLP is focused on changing the beliefs and sub modalities that hold us in our current behaviour patterns. This chapter is written with the presumption that you are happy with terms such as sub modalities (p.68), break state (p.87) and anchoring (p.86): if not re-read the relevant sections.

Major changework

With more significant issues, perhaps where a horse or rider was injured, a combination of techniques and processes need to be used. In these cases a one-to-one session with a fully qualified NLP Master Practitioner would be more effective than working from this book alone. Also where you want to make significant changes, which may involve exploring previous negative memories and limiting beliefs, it is often helpful to work with a Master Practitioner who is experienced in working therapeutically with people. This is because where people have a strongly held belief – that they can't do something, for instance – their unconscious mind will find a way to ensure that this remains true or to demonstrate that their behaviour is justified. Working through these smoke screens can thus require more expertise.

Tips for guiding a friend through these techniques

- Maintain rapport throughout.

- Really listen to your friend's memories and dreams rather than discussing them or adding in your own experiences. Otherwise the process will turn into a chat, with lots of content but little change.

- Accept whatever your friend says without making or expressing judgement on it. This is called having unconditional regard.

- Practise the sub modality questions (p.71) until you can use them without looking at the list.

- Listen for the different patterns, such as meta-programmes (p.32) or VAK language (p.71), to decide which questions to use.

- Check out the section on positive language and reframing (pp.60–66). It is needed throughout changework.

- Use second and third position skills (see p.96) to understand their experience from different perspectives.

- Most importantly, remember that your role is to leave your friend in a better state than when you started.

Exercise 33: Six-step reframing

This is a simple, playful and yet very powerful technique for addressing many problems and situations, particularly where you find yourself tripping yourself up with negative behaviour. It requires establishing a communication channel with the 'part' of you that is responsible for giving the negative response and discovering why it is doing it. The steps are as follows:

1 Find a quiet space and time, and think about the behaviour you want to change.

2 Set up communication with the part of you that is responsible for the behaviour. Ask this part to give you a signal that it will communicate with you. Pay attention to any internal images, feelings or words that you experience after you ask – these are the signals. Check that it feels alright to continue.

3 Think about the issue and then ask 'What is that doing for me?' or 'What is your positive intent?' Some ideas and comments will come out. It is helpful to write these down.

4 Call up the creative part or negotiating part of yourself and ask it to come up with three suggestions that satisfy the positive intention of the first part's behaviour, but do not have its negative consequences.

5 Ask the part that creates the negative behaviour whether it will agree to implement the new choices. Ask it to signal if it accepts the alternative choices. If any choices are not acceptable, or there is no signal, go back to step 3 and modify the choices. This may be a circular phase involving negotiating new behaviour with the original part until it is 'happy' with its new role. In NLP this is called an ecology check.

6 Finally, imagine a future scenario that would previously have caused the old behaviour and notice the differences. It may be appropriate to anchor (p.87) the new feeling.

Case study: No more panic attacks

case study

Most people are intrigued to realise how their tripping-up behaviour is all about protecting them, especially in health issues, but often it goes too far.

Debbie was having panic attacks out riding. Through the six-step reframing exercise, she discovered that the part of her that produced these attacks 'knew' she tended to be dreamy and slow to react, so it put her on a full-alert that went too far! By changing her routes, going out with another person and being more aware when she rode, she was able to reduce the panics. Later she moved to a more suitable yard.

The move meant she could have more relaxed riding, on a better network of bridleways.

Exercise 34:
The Swish Technique

The Swish Technique acts by bringing in the new desired way of behaving every time you start to do the old habit. It is a powerful route for changing habitual behaviour, but is less suitable for changing beliefs. When used in conjunction with belief change-work, however, it can make a powerful impact because it shows that the behaviours are different, as well as the beliefs. For instance, when I first learnt about NLP it coincided with the realisation that instead of being able to eat like a horse and stay slim, the weight was beginning to stay on. I used the Swish Technique to great effect to change my attitude to eating – see below.

1　First, identify the cue picture; this is the picture of you doing what you want to stop doing – the unappealing you. Be associated: seeing what you would do, feeling what you would feel, hearing what you would hear. Let the unpleasant aspects of this behaviour become even more intense by boosting the sub modalities.

2　Break state out of this memory.

3　Imagine what you would like to be like – the 'desirable' you. Adjust all the sub modalities until the picture is really attractive, noticing your expression, your posture, what you would be saying and hearing, and what you would be feeling like. It should be a realistic you, a you that you can believe in now. Optimise the sub modalities until the new you seems really alive, bright and in colour. Make it a picture that you want to be just like.

4　Take this image of the desirable you and imagine shrinking it down to be a tiny picture, no larger than a dot. Practise making it life-size again, then back to a tiny picture.

5　Recreate the first cue picture, the unappealing you image, as a big and bright picture. In the bottom left, put the second picture as a small, dark dot. Now, as fast as you can, swap the two over. If you are working with a friend they would do a fast 'swish' gesture towards your face at this point, making a suitable noise, which adds to the impact of the process.

6　Repeat this swapping over process three to four more times, doing it as fast as you can, and spending a few seconds enjoying the sensation of the new desirable you image in all its dimensions.

When you have run through the Swish Technique several times, test the effect by noticing what happens and how you feel when you try to run the original unappealing you image. The process has been effective when you cannot hold the picture without thinking of the new desirable you.

In my example, the positive image I used was to visualise and imagine feeling my riding jacket swinging loosely around my waist as I turned in the saddle towards the next jump. The unappealing cue picture was that ever-tempting forkful of high-calorie food, coming up to meet my lips. Using this simple process I found that I could eat when hungry, but was much more aware of when I had had enough. Instead of automatically having an extra helping, I would see myself on the horse, feel the jacket swinging and, knowing that this was important to me, just say no. As a result, I lost 10lbs without dieting and competed the next season looking much more elegant.

Case study: Ginny regains her confidence

Ginny explains how one NLP session including the Swish Technique helped her start enjoy riding her horse again.

'I'd had my previous horse until she was 26 and knew her like the back of my hand. As she got older I did less and less, but then I bought a 7-year old, 14.3hh piebald show cob. However, I'd forgotten what it feels like to ride a young fit horse, and although there isn't a nasty bone in his body, he soon found that he could intimidate me by bucking and cantering off to evade work. My confidence was shattered.'

Ginny took the cob to her instructor to sell him. But the instructor suggested they have another try at putting the partnership together. However, even after the horse had been reschooled, Ginny was still reluctant to canter on her own because the question in the back of her mind was whether he would buck or not – and occasionally he did because she was riding him so tensely.

Ginny continues 'I needed help to develop the confidence to ride, and I realised it had to come from me. The NLP session really changed my outlook towards my riding. Liz was sympathetic but still challenged my beliefs. When I said I was scared of riding, she pinned me down to understand exactly what it was I was afraid of – it was of my horse bucking and then running away with me in an open space. **She made me laugh as we discussed what the horse felt like** (Metaphors, p.64) **and I realised that the number of times this had happened were few compared to the number of times I had enjoyed a canter in the past!**

Then we imagined being someone else watching me with my fear, where I had to suggest what 'Ginny' could do to feel more secure and confident. With that part of the exercise I identified the 'safety nets' that I could put in place to feel better about cantering out. These included continuing my regular lessons, losing weight and becoming fitter so that I was in better balance, wearing a body protector and making sure someone knew what I was doing when I went out for a hack.

Having imagined everything in place, it seemed easy so I stepped in and became 'me' in the visualisation. Liz reinforced it with the Swish Technique, which felt very strange, like hurtling into the unknown, yet was a really lovely feeling as the new happy, confident behaviour took over from the old one. Then I could really believe that I could enjoy cantering across a field again!

The test came a week or so later. At the end of Ginny's lesson, her instructor commented, 'Do you know you didn't ask me if he'd buck today!'

Her instructor said, 'Ginny had had a panicky experience and was then remembering it as even worse than it actually was. At one stage, I even had to lead her around the school in walk. **In the lesson after the course we were in the field and I asked her if she wanted to canter and she just said "Yes" and did it. It has given her a much more positive attitude and this has in turn given her even more confidence.'**

Ginny explained what it felt like to canter with confidence. 'In the lesson, it hadn't entered my head that he might buck, yet up until then I'd always worried about it. And of course now he doesn't feel that I'm afraid, he's not so inclined to play up. Even if he does a little buck I'll be able to keep it in proportion so it shouldn't be a problem.'

'Two months later, I've lost 21lbs, I'm cantering in the fields and have hacked him out on my own – I'm even hoping to ride him at a show myself. That one session has helped me to take charge of myself, and is another positive step towards regaining my confidence.'

Exercise 35:
The Phobia Cure

Whenever I am present in an accident situation, such as a fall or a horse standing on someone's foot, I use the Phobia Cure, a technique that has been adopted by several accident and emergency teams around the world. It disassociates the mind from the event so rewriting it for the person involved and reducing the long-term harmful effects.

This method was developed to work with more intense fears or phobias, such as spiders or being in enclosed spaces. However, I recommend that you learn the process thoroughly first, using a more moderate situation.

1 Take a minute and think of a moderately negative memory. It could be a minor fall or an incident like the horse treading on your foot. Think about it enough to get a little bit of the flavour of the feeling.

2 Now imagine you are sitting in front of a large TV. See yourself on the screen in a disassociated, detached way, just before the incident happened, and then see it happening, small, in black and white and slow motion, you can even make it on a poor quality, scratchy film. Watch until you reach the end of the situation when the trauma was over, and you can tell from your film that you are safe again.

3 Stop the film at the end. Imagine stepping into the still picture on the screen and going through the experience backwards, in full colour, just as if time were reversed and you were being sucked into a giant vacuum cleaner, back to before it happened. Do this very quickly, in about two or three seconds. Repeat this step several more times. By doing this sequence 3–4 times, the mind will disassociate you from the incident.

4 When you're finished, physically get up and move around. Shake your arms. Take deep breaths.

5 When you think about the memory now it should be quite different, even difficult to recall. Next think about the situation, imagining what you could have done differently, making it a near-miss rather than an accident. Run through it as if it were happening on the TV again: small, black and white, and so on, until you can believe it. Then step into the memory and see what you would have seen under these better and different circumstances, feel what you would have felt and put more positive sounds and words in.

TIP

It is important to find the point at which you would have done something differently, it could even be sometime earlier. One client found that she would have sent the horse back to its former owner as soon as she realised it wasn't suitable.

Case study: Carol clears a bad memory

Carol and I worked through this exercise to help her clear a memory about a collecting ring incident where the horse she was riding spooked and landed on a pushchair.

Luckily no one was hurt, but she just couldn't stop thinking about what might have happened. **We went through the Phobia Cure process thoroughly, which cleared the event.** In particular, Carol realised how important it was to work in well so her horse was not too fresh when it was asked to stand in the collecting ring. In the 'near miss' run-through at the end, she had her horse being attentive to her and she politely asked the family with the pushchair to move it away from the ring entrance. **We made sure that the sub modality changes were emphasised, so that the original haunting image was really minimized.** We then added a process where she thought about how she would respond differently – what she had learnt. Finally, we anchored a calm, resourceful feeling.

see also:
Sub modalities
pp.67–78
Reframing pp.62–63

After our session, Carol was able to get back to riding well again, just as she wanted to.

Exercise 36: Integrating conflicting beliefs

Where people tend to think negatively about themselves, there is often a conflict in their belief systems. This leads to contradictory behaviour, which in turn creates a what is called a double bind – where you are 'damned if you do and damned if you don't'. An example is someone wanting to do well in competition then behaving in ways that undermine their performance by forgetting their test or the course, for instance, or by arriving late or simply suddenly becoming very tense and nervous when it is their turn. Integrating conflicting beliefs is a commonly used technique and is very effective. However, six-step reframing or others may also be appropriate. Read Jay's case study (opposite) to get an understanding of how it works before you try it out. It is helpful to have a friend take you through these steps.

1 With the help of your friend's questions (see pp.42–43), identify the two key conflicting beliefs.

2 Take these and imagine them as it they were two different identities, then identify the critical sub modalities (see p.74) to boost the images you get. Your friend can help by asking, for example, 'What images, voices and feelings do you associate with that part of you?' for each identity.

3 Give these two identities a personality. For instance, one could be you in work mode, the other in relaxed and lazy mode, or they could be an older and younger you. I have also had people imagining them as wizards; they could also be symbols like red balls and floaty clouds, too. Whatever springs to mind is fine. Now imagine putting the part of you that believes X in one hand. Put the other part, Y, in the other hand.

4 Ask each part, X and Y, to look at the other and describe what it sees. At this stage, they will typically dislike and distrust each other.

5 Find out what the positive intention and purpose of each part is by asking each in turn. Make sure that each part then recognises and accepts the positive intent of the other. Use the logical levels (p.46) to step up to the higher levels of intent, until you get agreement.

6 Make sure each part realises that the conflict is directly interfering with the achievement of its own purposes. Have them look at each other again and this time ask each to describe the resources that the other has that would be helpful to them. Ask each to verbalise what new beliefs they would choose as a result.

7 Work out an agreement between the parts about how, by combining resources, they can more fully achieve both their purposes. Usually this will be around a core reason that they will have mistrusted or disliked each other previously. At this point, other limiting beliefs that have not surfaced previously may appear: they will need to be refined or updated, by working through them in the same way.

8 When all the parts have been reconciled, bring your hands together so that each part fully clasps the other. This creates a new representation of their identities that fully integrates the resources of both parts in all sensory systems. Sometimes a conflict may involve more than two identity issues. If there are three, expand this technique to include all three; if there are more do the integrations two at a time.

Case study: Jay makes a choice

Jay had got to the point where he simply could not sort out his problem on his own. He had the opportunity to work abroad – a good job in Australia starting racehorses – yet could not decide whether to go because he kept thinking about the need to stay around for his elderly father and his sisters.

The outcome process identified that this was the issue, but it could not be fully concluded once his conflict was identified, so we moved into changework on it.

The first identity to come out was his late mother, worrying about who would look after the family. This was quite an odd sensation for Jay, as he tended to deny this caring side. **The other identity was a young and ambitious Jay, wanting to get out in the world for himself.** When the 'ambitious' identity came out, it did not even want to look the 'mother' identity in the eye. As the process developed Jay's 'mother' realised that, in fact, the family would be more secure (the resource she needed) if he went off to develop his career. The ambitious identity

realised that it needed the support of the family in order for Jay to 'keep his roots alive'. Bringing these conflicting parts together then came easily as he promised to keep in close touch with the family. He was now able to complete the outcome process and clarify what he wanted.

see also:
The outcome
process p.14

A couple of years later the family had all enjoyed staying with Jay in Australia and then his job developed into flying all around the world with top Thoroughbreds, so he was able to visit home quite regularly.

Exercise 37:
Re-imprinting

Re-imprinting helps you to find the resources necessary to change and update limiting beliefs or clusters of beliefs that were imprinted at an early age. It involves metaphorically going back in time to the experience which made you form those beliefs. It often involves the unconscious role-modelling of other people who were important to you.

Using time to make changes is a valuable technique. Think about a memory as a single picture or snapshot. Gather a selection of them, put them into date order and imagine them stacked in a line going away from you, with the oldest memory the furthest away. Equally imagine some pictures of your dreams and things happening in the future, the most immediate being closest to you. This is the basis of the timeline concept, which is used in a number of NLP techniques, one of the most powerful being re-imprinting. The steps to re-imprinting are only summarised here as it is most helpful to be taken through the process by an experienced NLP Master Practitioner.

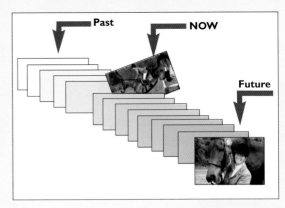

1 Identify the specific feelings, as well as words or images, associated with the limiting belief. Most people want to avoid these feelings because they are uncomfortable. However, remember that avoiding them won't resolve the limitation.

2 Stay with the feeling and remember back to the earliest experience of the feeling associated with the impasse. Tell your partner the generalisations or beliefs that were formed from the experience.

3 Disassociate yourself from the experience by imagining you are watching a film of yourself. Find the positive intent or the benefit of the feeling of limitation. Where there are other people involved in the memory, find the positive intention of their behaviour as well. This may be done by imagining asking the people you see in the memory what they wanted in the situation.

4 You can now check what resources (p.86) were missing. Having identified them, briefly anchor (p.87) those resources you needed but did not have then, but do have now. This may be anything: calmness, trust, self belief or simply the ability to say you did not know. Imagine giving these resources to the younger you, and the other people as gifts. They should thank you for them, too.

5 For each of the people involved in the memory, replay the film from their perspective to see how the experience would have changed if the necessary resources had been available to that character then; keep the behaviour of the others as it was at that time. After the resources have been added, say what new generalisations or beliefs you would choose as a result.

6 Make sure the resources you identified really would be sufficient to change the experience. If not, go back to the previous steps and identify other positive intentions and/or resources that may have been overlooked.

7 Re-live the imprint experience from the point of view of each of the people involved one at a time, incorporating the needed resource. Finish with your own perspective at the time. Run through the new experience until it is as strong as the original imprint.

8 State the new or modified beliefs you would now take from the experience.

Case studies: David becomes more confident

David was finding that he kept losing his nerve when riding to fences cross country, particularly down hill.

When we went through the re-imprinting process, he remembered that at about eight or nine years old, he had wanted to ride and had had just a couple of lessons. He boasted of his abilities to his friends, one of whom, Peter, had a couple of ponies. The two boys told Peter's parents that David could ride, and they kindly offered to let him ride out with their son. **The boys went off, and almost inevitably the ride ended with the pony taking off in a favourite canter place and the young David ending in a heap on the floor.** No damage was done except a significant blow to his pride and the indignity of both sets of parents telling him off for being so boastful.

All was forgotten for many years until David came to me for help with his jumping confidence. We discovered that the problem extended to insecurity about tackling new things in other areas of his adult life, too. He spontaneously went back to this incident. **The resources he realised he needed were an awareness of his ability, and that it was acceptable to admit he was not knowledgeable, even when among his peers.**

When we went back to the incident and 'gave' the resources to the young him, he could see and hear himself explaining how much he had actually ridden, and, of course, the whole episode changed: Peter's parents stayed nearby, David and Peter did not canter and David did not fall off.

David realised it was OK for his younger self to want to learn alongside a more experienced friend. He also realised he could work to improve his current position to give him security when jumping downhill.

By bringing this learning back into the present, he was able to feel more relaxed and positive about his cross-country riding.

Bibliography & Further Reading

Horsemanship, NLP and personal development are vibrant and generous communities with many interrelated ideas. It is therefore difficult to accredit precisely where the original concepts and exercises came from. Included here are books referenced in the text, any that were the sources of some of the ideas for exercises, and those that have influenced my thinking over the past years.

Horsemanship

Riding Towards the Light, Paul Belasik (JA Allen 1990)

Exploring Dressage Technique, Paul Belasik (JA Allen 1994)

The Art of Training, Hans von Blixen-Finecke (Kenilworth Press 1996)

The Art of Dressage, Alois Podhajsky (Harrap 1976)

Dressage Priority Points, Richard Davison (Regency House Publishing 1995)

Goodwood Dressage Champions, Jane Kidd (Kenilworth Press 1994)

Jumping is Jumping, Jane Wallace (Methuen 1994)

Training Show Jumpers, Anthony Paalman (JA Allen 1984)

The de Nemethy Method, Bertalan de Nemethy (Partridge Press 1990)

So Far So Good, The Autobiography, Mark Todd (Weidenfeld & Nicholson 1998)

A Good Horse is Never a Bad Color, Mark Rashid (Spring Creek Press 1996)

Horses Never Lie, Mark Rashid (Johnson Books 2000)

The Nature of Horses, Stephen Budiansky (Weidenfeld & Nicholson 1997)

Savvy System Parts 1-3, Pat Parelli (Parelli Natural Horse.Man.Ship 1999)

Related Interest

Healing for Horses, Margrit Coates (*Rider*/Ebury Press 2001)

The Veterinary Care of the Horse, Liz Morrison & Sue Devereux (JA Allen 1992)

A Natural History of the Senses, Diane Ackerman (Chapmans 1990)

Kinship with All Life, J. Allen Boone (Harper Row O/P)

Neuro Linguistic Programming

NLP, the New Technology of Achievement, Steve Andreas & Charles Faulkner (Nicholas Brearley Publishing 1996)

Reframing, Richard Bandler & John Grinder (Real People Press 1982)

Using your Brain for a Change, Richard Bandler (Real People Press 1985)

Time for a Change, Richard Bandler (Meta Publications 1993)

Beliefs – Pathways to health & well-being, Robert Dilts, Tim Hallbom & Suzi Smith (Metamorphous Press 1990)

Introducing NLP, John Seymour & Joseph O'Connor (Thorsons 1993)

Words that Change Minds, Shelley Rose Charvet (Kendall Hunt 1997)

Awaken the Giant Within, Anthony Robbins (Simon & Schuster 1991)

NLP at Work, Sue Knight (Nicholas Brearley 1995)

Modelling with NLP, Robert Dilts (Meta Publications 1988)

Therapeutic Metaphors, David Gordon (Meta Publications 1978)

Influencing with Integrity, Genie Laborde (Syntony 1983)

The Secret of Creating your Future, Tad James (Advanced Neuro Dynamics 1989)

Sports Psychology and Personal Development

The Seven Habits of Highly Effective People, Stephen Covey (Simon & Schuster 1992)

Piece of Mind, Sandy MacGregor (CALM 1993)

NLP & Sport, Joseph O'Connor (Thorsons 2001)

That Winning Feeling, Jane Savoie (JA Allen 1998)

Gold Minds, Brian Miller (Crowood Press 1997)

Learning more about NLP

Many courses, workshops and forums about the applications of NLP are held around the world. Visit my website sportingtactics.co.uk for links to individuals and training companies I have personally experienced and can recommend.

It is my belief that in order to 'get in the muscle' sufficient to work congruently with clients it is necessary to complete at least a full 20 day Practitioner and then a 20 day Master Practitioner accredited training course, which are usually spread over 6-9 months each to allow time for course work and projects. The shorter intensive courses use hypnotic learning techniques and are excellent for those seeking a powerful personal experience but are unlikely to provide the same depth of understanding.

About the Author

Liz Morrison is a licensed NLP Master Practitioner who applies the powerful techniques of NLP to her work as a Sports Coach and International Level 2 Riding Instructor, as well as in Business. She works with sports people across all disciplines. Her positive and energetic style is enhanced with the use of humour, one of the main reasons why her approach is so popular. Her courses about applying NLP to riding, sport and generally 'life' have been attended by hundreds of participants and their coaches around the country. She is also a regular feature writer in the biggest selling UK equestrian magazines.

She first became aware of the importance of mental attitude in sport when she was awarded a Winston Churchill Memorial Trust Travelling Fellowship to Australia in 1993. What she noted in her three-month visit was the Australian's determination and openness about doing whatever was necessary to improve and win. It was this that led to their success. Upon her return to the UK she researched the area and started training in NLP. She has trained with the all of original developers of the subject, and now assists on their training sessions in the UK.

She lives in West Sussex, UK and owns two horses that she competes in affiliated dressage and show jumping. She is also co-author of *The Veterinary Care of the Horse* with Sue Devereux, hardback published by JA Allen (Robert Hale Group) in 1993.

Your Steps to Riding Success Now

Liz has some availability to work one to one with individuals, and is also building a network of appropriately trained NLP practitioners. If you would like information about this network, or her courses and lectures for riders, competitors, teams and sports coaches visit the website: sportingtactics.co.uk or email: lizmorrison@ontel.net.uk. You can also write to:

Sporting Tactics
PO Box 177
Billingshurst, West Sussex,
RH14 0YW, UK.

Index

Acknowledgements

The Winston Churchill Memorial Trust, whose support in providing a Travelling Fellowship to Australia started my learning about positive attitude and the power of the mind.

My teachers who have inspiration in the art and science of NLP over the years including: Richard Bandler, Judith Delozier, Robert Dilts, Charles Faulkner, David Gordon, Christina Hall, Judith Lowe, Joseph O'Connor Julian Russell and John Seymour.

My teachers in horsemanship over the years including: Lynne Baldwin, Rob Hoekstra, Pammy Hutton, Bill Noble, Sally Thurloway, John Tuff and Bertil Voss.

The friends who have inspired and supported me in the writing of this book: Richard, Tony & Jenny, Sue, Peta, Helen, Carrie & Brian, Chris & Roger, and especially my parents, who not only provided a Scottish base, free of all distractions, to write but also prepared the index.

The team at David & Charles: Jane Trollope, Sue Cleave, Tom McCann and Jo Weeks for their belief and investment in the idea – and patience in producing the result.

And finally to my pupils and clients from whom I have learned at first hand and whose feedback has provided the momentum to continue.